Praise for *I'll Seize the Day Tomorrow* and Jonathan Goldstein

"Jonathan Goldstein is one of today's most original and intelligent comic voices. He has done for radio what Larry David has done for television. And in his new book he proves, once again, that his wry, self-deprecating observations work just as well on the page."

—David Bezmozgis, author of *Natasha and Other Stories* and *The Free World*

"Jonathan Goldstein has created something uniquely funny, smart, and touching. I love this book."

—Neil Pasricha, author of the *New York Times* bestseller *The Book of Awesome*

"Surrounded by [Goldstein's] cast of family and friends, this chronicle of his 39th year is a portrait of a life that is striving towards hope and beauty—even wisdom—against the relentless pull of the gravity that is one's own character, and the entropy that is age ... I smiled or laughed at every page."

—Sheila Heti, author of *How Should a Person Be?*

"One of the funniest books I've read in a long time. Jonathan is like a mix of Louis C.K., Jean-Paul Sartre, and Sholem Aleichem. I guess what I'm trying to say is that he's hilarious, philosophical, and Jewish. I want to be Jonathan Goldstein when I turn 40. (Note: I'm 44, but you know what I mean)."

—A.J. Jacobs, author of the *New York Times* bestseller *The Year of Living Biblically*

"Jonathan Goldstein's existential misery makes for good reading. As long as he keeps writing such funny and original pieces about it, I hope he continues to suffer."

—Shalom Auslander, author of *Foreskin's Lament*

"*I'll Seize the Day Tomorrow* is packed with Goldstein's trademark combo of sharp-edged wit and tender wisdom. It's his funniest book yet!"

—Miriam Toews, author of *A Complicated Kindness*

"With his brilliant deadpan and his all-seeing eye, the hilarious Jonathan Goldstein traffics in what he calls 'moderate hopefulness.' It fills me with wild optimism."

—Henry Alford, author of *Would It Kill You To Stop Doing That?*

"Jonathan Goldstein is one of the funniest and most original writers I can think of. Anything by him is better than anything by just about anyone else."

—David Sedaris, author of the *New York Times* bestsellers *Me Talk Pretty One Day* and *When You Are Engulfed in Flames*

"Jonathan Goldstein is like no one else. He's constantly surprising, simultaneously poetic and hilarious; an honest-to-goodness artist."

—David Rakoff, bestselling author of *Don't Get Too Comfortable*

PENGUIN

I'LL SEIZE THE DAY TOMORROW

JONATHAN GOLDSTEIN's writing has appeared in *The New York Times Magazine*, *GQ*, and *Nerve*. He is a columnist for the *National Post* and a frequent contributor to PRI's *This American Life*. He's the author of the short story collection *Ladies and Gentlemen, The Bible!* and the novel *Lenny Bruce Is Dead*. His CBC Radio show, *WireTap*, is now in its ninth season.

ALSO BY JONATHAN GOLDSTEIN

Lenny Bruce Is Dead
Ladies and Gentlemen, The Bible!

I'LL SEIZE THE DAY TOMORROW

JONATHAN GOLDSTEIN

PENGUIN
an imprint of Penguin Canada

Published by the Penguin Group
Penguin Group (Canada),
90 Eglinton Avenue East, Suite 700, Toronto, Ontario, Canada M4P 2Y3

Penguin Group (USA) Inc., 375 Hudson Street, New York, New York 10014, U.S.A.
Penguin Books Ltd, 80 Strand, London WC2R 0RL, England
Penguin Ireland, 25 St Stephen's Green, Dublin 2, Ireland
(a division of Penguin Books Ltd)
Penguin Group (Australia), 250 Camberwell Road, Camberwell, Victoria 3124, Australia
(a division of Pearson Australia Group Pty Ltd)
Penguin Books India Pvt Ltd, 11 Community Centre, Panchsheel Park,
New Delhi – 110 017, India
Penguin Group (NZ), 67 Apollo Drive, Rosedale, Auckland 0632, New Zealand
(a division of Pearson New Zealand Ltd)
Penguin Books (South Africa) (Pty) Ltd, 24 Sturdee Avenue, Rosebank,
Johannesburg 2196, South Africa

Penguin Books Ltd, Registered Offices: 80 Strand, London WC2R 0RL, England

First published 2012

1 2 3 4 5 6 7 8 9 10 (WEB)

Manufactured in Canada.

LIBRARY AND ARCHIVES CANADA CATALOGUING IN PUBLICATION

Goldstein, Jonathan, 1969–
I'll seize the day tomorrow / Jonathan Goldstein.

ISBN 978-0-14-317388-5

1. Goldstein, Jonathan, 1969– —Humor. I. Title.

PS8563.O82846I55 2012   C817'.6   C2012-905314-7

Visit the Penguin Canada website at **www.penguin.ca**

Special and corporate bulk purchase rates available; please see
www.penguin.ca/corporatesales or call 1-800-810-3104, ext. 2477.

ALWAYS LEARNING   PEARSON

For my family and friends, past and present.
And what the heck, I'm feeling good:
for those, too, who may not even like me,
because they might some day.
Who knows. Life is weird.

Contents

Foreword

by Gregor Ehrlich, agent to the star

One wintry morning many years ago, my butler opened the door of my *maison de campagne* and discovered a basket of reeds with a baby inside. There was a note pinned to the swaddling cloth explaining that the baby's name was Jonathan Goldstein, who, due to an unspecified condition, had been born well on the other side of his prime. Here was a middle-aged-man baby. And one who had not lived well at that. He was doughy, rotund, and bald—and not baby bald, but Ed Asner bald. In fact, the only thing baby-like about this creature were his genitals. Which were small.

I gave him the finest education money could buy. Elocution. Archery. Japanese stick fighting. And finally the day came to send young Goldstein out into the world—a hero's quest for my little hero! He was to fetch my dry cleaning. I'd lost the slip, but hoped he could get my pants anyway.

Unable to explain the situation to the proprietor, he threw a veritable conniption, carrying on in the shop about everything and nothing. But as Lady Luck would have it, a talent scout for the Canadian Broadcasting Corporation happened to be *in that very dry cleaning establishment* and heard in Goldstein's high-pitched hysterical mewling something universal. Here was a voice—a cross between Joe Franklin trying to sing through his nose and the panicky shrieks of Larry King awakening during a hernia operation—that would one day touch the lives of hundreds.

And so his radio show, *WireTap*, was born. Although I've not heard it, I'm told Goldstein uses his governmentally funded half-hour to perform monologues about everything from his corns to his cankles, occasionally mixing it up with a modern-day fable obtuse enough to put knots in a rabbinical scholar's beard.

For the next eight years I would try unsuccessfully to pry Goldstein off that stupid show. But cling he does, like a barnacle on the underbelly of a ship, a ship he calls "Show Business"—a glorious place where Ed McMahon spits bingo numbers and Frank Sinatra slaps his valet across the nose for rumpling his cabana wear.

From his radio show sprang his column in the *National Post*, where each week his writing sits proudly alongside word scrambles, terrible international tragedies, and *Marmaduke*. And those columns *led to this very book*.

"Pack it with sex," I advised. "Detailed anatomical descriptions of naked ladies sunbathing and such. Those without internet, i.e., the book-buying public at large, need nudity, too."

"It's my belief that fans of my work would rather read my *pensées* on everyday life," said Goldstein.

I'd like to apologize.

As a man with a Netflix account and an active social life, I've not had time to read this book, so I can't vouch for its worth. I'm told it represents a year in the life of Goldstein as he approaches his fortieth birthday and confronts his mortality. I *can* vouch for this foreword, though, which you are now enjoying immensely, because I have written it. I intend to also write the afterword, so that should be enough to keep you soldiering on to the end.

Perhaps it's best to think of this book as a sandwich. A sandwich made of delicious, crusty, fresh-baked bread. Smeared on this bread is something that tastes like, well, let's just keep this civil and say, I'll see you at the end.★

★Hummus.

Youth
(39th birthday)

MONDAY.

Before stepping out, I accidentally put my shoes on the wrong feet. It's something I haven't done since I was a kid. The sensation of my left shoe on my right foot makes me feel about six years old. It's like playing with ants, like sitting in a sunbeam on the carpet. Though we pretend otherwise, we're all our ages at once. I decide to start putting my shoes on the wrong feet whenever I need to remind myself of that. To this end, I will also take up skipping, though only late at night when no one is around. This, too, will make me feel young. But also insane.

THURSDAY.

It's close to midnight and tomorrow's my thirty-ninth birthday.

I wish you could leap from thirty-eight straight to forty. More dignity to it than hanging on to the last dregs of your thirties.

Forty was the age at which I thought I'd have a house full of oak shelves spilling over with hardcover books. Cabinets loaded with china. Carpets brought home from exotic trips abroad.

"Where'd these come from?" they'd ask.

"Abroad," I'd say.

The age at which I'd have a piano substantial enough to cripple the back of each member of the moving team that finally gets it into the upstairs parlour.

"Do you play?" they'd ask.

"I always wished I could," I always wished I could say.

Forty was supposed to be the age at which I'd have a gigantic flat-screen TV, one that sinks into the wall like a corrugated iron anchor. A wife. Kids. Peace, too. The kind that rises like mist from a settled life, the life of a man who's figured out the cologne that suits him and the channels he wants programmed into his car radio.

With all that in order, I'd be ready to do one of those Russian leg-kicking dances straight towards the grave with a smile on my face.

But here I am with no wife, no kids, no car, and no house. Not even a house*boat*. And the clever names I could have given one!

With so little to show for it, is it possible to even call myself a grownup?

I need to get my house in order. Man up and settle down. And the way I see it, I have one year left to do it.

This weekend will involve dinner with my parents and phone messages from my friends' kids singing "Happy Birthday." I'm sure it's just me, but every year the tone of their singing seems to get more mocking.

FRIDAY.

Step one: shave.

While doing so, I stop at the moustache and stare at myself in the mirror. Moustachioedness. I look like a completely different style of person, like the kind of guy who'd sing Motown songs in the public showers at the Y— someone who'd shirtlessly open his front door to the gas man, possibly calling him "chief."

When I finish I'm left feeling as if, after a long night out, my face has finally taken off its pants. But when Gregor stops by, he tells me I look older.

"I'm on public radio," I say. "It doesn't matter how I look. And for that matter, it's also why I don't need an agent."

"You already have that old-person smell," he says. "Hospital cafeteria. Hamburger steak in particular."

"I'm feeling a little sensitive about my age at the moment," I say, "so maybe lay off."

"By my math, you're thirty-nine going on dead," he says in his version of laying off. "You're aging out of your audience by the second. Do you think Millennials will tune in to hear about your latest visit to the doctor? And so I propose The Goldstein Pavilion, a section in Canada's Wonderland with rides based on your show. Stuff like the Monologue Monorail."

"Which would be?"

"A slow, meandering ride with no end in sight."

According to *Film World*, the secret to Fatty Arbuckle's success—what set him apart from other morbidly obese vaudevillians who could balance on telephone wires—was that he was possessed of an ability to laugh at himself. This is another in a long and growing list of reasons why I am nothing like Fatty Arbuckle. Nonetheless, as Gregor jokes, I try to laugh and my face takes on the expression of someone trying to lap up a saucer of pennies.

The way that people can learn so much personal information from looking at a face strikes me as unfair. Even a beard is not enough to cover up the truth of who you are.

The Things Left Undone
(52 weeks till 40th birthday)

SUNDAY.

My father is now on the internet and we've started emailing each other. The way it works is he sends me an email and then calls several seconds later to make sure I've received it, just in case.

For my father, a man who shows up at the airport five to six hours before departure—a man who fills his gas tank about every ten minutes—"just in case" are the three most important words in the English language. If we were the kind of family to have a crest, those words would be emblazoned in Latin across a figure of a man wearing a medicine ball–sized fanny pack.

I read his emails back to him over the phone.

"HI, JONNY," I read, "REPLY AS SOON AS YOU CAN AS I WANT TO SEE IF MY EMAIL IS WORKING."

"Unbelievable," he says. "I just sent it to you a second ago!"

I've also started sending him links to sites I think he might enjoy. Among them, *The Onion*.

"I read this op-ed piece," he says, "about a man who leaves behind instructions for what to do with his sandwich in case he dies before finishing it. Very poignant."

I try to explain that it's a joke, that *The Onion* is a satirical newspaper, not a real one, but my father won't buy it.

"It's poignant," he repeats. "It addresses one's sense of mortality and the legacy we wish to leave behind. The sandwich is a metaphor for the things left undone."

"What's the article called?" I ask.

"If I Die, Please Finish This Sandwich."

We argue for a while, but then I decide to drop the subject. His way of reading the paper might be better anyway. I can see the *Onion* headline: "Area Man Mistakes Humorous Weekly for Legitimate News Source."

MONDAY.

In my latest bid to multitask, I've begun screening silent films while listening to the radio. And so I watch Buster Keaton hop from train-car roof to train-car roof as a German scientist on the CBC explains how the Earth might one day be engulfed by the sun. The combined effect has me toggling between joy and existential terror. Not so different from how I feel most of the time, anyway.

The film is *The General* and it takes place during the American Civil War. In it, Keaton is trying to outrace the Unionists back to his base to alert the Confederate troops of a surprise attack.

As I watch, it strikes me how many movie plots would have been ruined if cell phones existed. I mean, all Keaton would've had to do was call ahead and let them know the army was coming and the whole film would have been over in five minutes. *Deliverance?* The war with the hillbillies would have been averted by a call to 911. *The Wizard of Oz?* They call up the wizard, and he's not home. The end.

The scientist on the radio is now describing what the Earth being consumed by fire would look like; although, he concedes, no one would actually get to see it happen, as human life would be long gone before then.

I get up and turn off the radio. Life's too short to attempt too much at once. I sink back into the couch and watch the rest of the film in silence.

FRIDAY.

Tony is driving me home from work. At the stoplight, he calls his fiancée, Natalie, on his cell phone.

"I'm on my way home," he says. "Need me to pick up hot dogs?"

Tony really likes hot dogs. Natalie doesn't. He listens for a while, says goodbye, and then turns to me.

"Her answer is always no," he says, "but I just can't stop trying."

Sometimes a cell phone can change life's course of events, but most of the time it's just as powerless as anything else.

Popeye Loves His Olives
(51 weeks)

TUESDAY.

I'm out for dinner with Marie-Claude, and after the waiter takes our order she stares at me appraisingly.

"A spinach salad?" she asks. "With cranberries and goat cheese?"

"I like spinach," I say, suddenly ashamed.

"I don't get you. Whatever happened to the Jonathan Goldstein who never felt a meal was complete without French fries?"

"He died of a heart attack at thirty-two."

The thing about having childhood friends is that they see any changes in your behaviour since the age of eleven as a betrayal of your basic personality. If you're not collecting hockey cards with a face covered in chocolate, you're a pretentious ass.

As a compromise, I consider eating the salad with my hands when it arrives.

WEDNESDAY.

I'm on my way to Waterloo, Ontario, to deliver a keynote address, and while waiting for the plane to board, I have a sandwich and beer at the airport bar. The tab comes to nearly seventeen dollars. After paying it, I look at the bill.

While I'm irked that the bartender has bundled a service fee into the total, I'm galled that the additional tip I just paid him was calculated based on that total—a total that included a gratuity I'd been unwittingly bilked out of.

Just as I'm about to say something—or, rather, just as I'm about to *consider* saying something—the bartender approaches me with a large jar of olives.

"I've been trying to open it all evening," he says, his face red with exertion. "Would you mind trying?"

His request catches me off guard. In an instant I go from feeling angry to feeling needed. I attack the jar with the kind of ferocious determination that involves grunting, grimacing, and almost herniating my disc. For some inexplicable reason, I want nothing more than to prove myself to a complete stranger who, only moments earlier, ripped me off.

After about a minute, the lid pops open. I'm covered in sweat and olive juice. The bartender thanks me and then, for a job well done, hands me a plastic shot glass full of olives.

As I walk away eating olives and feeling grateful, it strikes me that the bartender's gesture could very easily be employed in other ticklish social situations. Newspaper vendor treating you brusquely? Office manager doesn't say hello in the elevator? Friend thinks your choice of healthy appetizer makes you seem too high and mighty? Just pull a jar of olives out and ask for help. Call it "extending the olive jar."

FRIDAY.

Flying back to Montreal after my talk, I grab some air sickness bags to use for packing work lunches. Not only will looking at them work as a natural appetite suppressant, but they might also discourage anyone from stealing my lunch from the refrigerator.

Why a Duck?
(50 weeks)

MONDAY.

The janitor has emptied the garbage can in my office a day early. It's a small thing, but it's still a break from the routine. I'm reminded of the day in grade three when Eddy Kaplan showed up in the lunchroom with a sandwich made with green bread. Eddy's mother was different from the other mothers—into meditating and yoga—and she'd dyed his bread with green food colouring. It wasn't St. Patrick's Day or anything. She just wanted to remind him, and everyone else at the cafeteria table, that when you unexpectedly break from the routine, you are reawakened to the possibilities around you.

I look at my trash can, its emptiness one day early and so full of possibility that I hardly know where to start.

TUESDAY.

Josh has just returned from a trip to upstate New York. He says the best part was buying roadside pot pies. In the area of pot pies, he says he now has two pieces of wisdom: "One, when given the opportunity, always take the duck pot pie; and two, the more decrepit the sign at the side of the road, the better the pie."

He then tells me about a place where the sign on the lawn looked hand-drawn by a hillbilly with a broken arm. When he rang the doorbell, he was greeted by an old woman wearing what appeared to be a hospital gown. She looked as though he had woken her out of a deep sleep. She invited him in and prepared him pies while he sat waiting at her kitchen table.

"I ordered the duck," he says, "and I never looked back."

I nod my head and Josh repeats "duck pie" over and over, as if the words are filled with magic.

WEDNESDAY.

I've been experimenting with colognes lately, trying to find one that could become my signature odour. I don't know how people make such a choice. It's like choosing your eye colour. It feels too big, something that should be left to the deity. Nonetheless, I've become rather fond of Gucci. To my mind, it makes me smell like the inside of a rich old man's toiletry bag.

As I walk to the store with Marie-Claude's kids—my goddaughters, nine-year-old Helen and seven-year-old Katie—they complain about my smell.

"I like the way you stink normal," Katie says.

"Yes," I say, "but my normal stink is too subtle." Plus, I explain to her, by leaving a heavily odorous trail, we'll be sure to find our way back home more easily.

"Like Hansel and Gretel with the bread crumbs," I assure her.

This gets Helen thinking.

"I never could understand why that witch was so excited about eating kids," she says. "She could have just eaten a chicken."

Helen will come to learn that everyone, even witches, likes a little break from routine. That's why there are not only chicken pot pies but duck pot pies, as well.

THURSDAY.

Outside my window, I hear the sound of the garbage truck advancing and, as always, I am filled with a low hum of anxiety. Even if my garbage is already out on the curb, there's always a part of me that views the approaching truck as a chance to throw one last dunk shot into oblivion. Though not hungry, I'm tempted to force-feed myself a banana just for the opportunity to barrel out the door and rid the household of the peel. For me, a garbage truck is a hybrid between an empty work trash can and the ice cream man.

As I scan the apartment for potential garbage—water-logged stacks of business cards, empty CD cases, notebooks full of ideas I'll never realize—everything becomes bathed in the aura of trash.

I've always wanted to feel like my life was rife with potential, but now, as the garbage truck outside grows louder, it only feels rife with potential garbage.

Survival of the Fittest
(49 weeks)

SUNDAY.

I'm taking my father shopping for a TV. As we leave his house, he says goodbye to his new dog, Boosh, short for Babushka. Although he calls her his "rescue poodle," it seems too Super Heroic a name for a dog that spends twenty-three hours of the day sleeping, and the remaining hour eating venison dog food and being cuddled.

My father hands her over to me.

"Say goodbye to your sister," he says. Calling Boosh my sister is my father's new favourite joke. I don't know how my human sister feels about having a new dog sibling, or my mother feels about having a new dog daughter, but personally, I'm not loving it. My new sister growls in my face and I hand her back.

"Doesn't she do any tricks?" I ask in the car. "Anything to earn her keep?"

"The SPCA didn't know much about her previous owners," he says, "but I'm learning of her talents all the time. Like the other day, I was arguing with your mother …"

"About what?" I ask.

"She has a habit of handing me peeled bananas, and it drives me nuts. You can't refuse a banana that's already been peeled."

"Why not?"

"It just isn't done," he says. "So I might be in the middle of shellacking a bookcase or shovelling snow when all of a sudden, there's the banana. I have to drop everything and start eating before it goes black. It's very manipulative. Anyway, in the middle of the yelling, Boosh started yipping!"

"Talented," I say.

"All rescue dogs have a talent," he says. "For staying alive."

"At any rate they're lucky," I say.

Maybe we all are. Each of us evolved from the sperm that made it—that beat out the millions of others—and for that, we're all at least sort of lucky. And we're all, if maybe only occasionally, seized with a bit of that "I'm lucky to be alive" feeling. Maybe even dogs are.

TUESDAY.

At work, my producer, Mira, informs me that fat raccoons are taking over Mount Royal.

"They really know how to play an audience for hand-outs, too," she says. "When they see you walking by, they start scooping water with their paws and look up at you all cute. But I can see through them."

I believe this statement says more about Mira than it does about the raccoons on Mount Royal.

WEDNESDAY.

I get a new picture taken for my security card at work. When I sit down to pose for it, I decide that, in spite of the bad day I'm having, I'm going to make an effort to smile. The picture is snapped and I'm handed my pass.

There isn't a trace of a smile. I look like mug-shot Nick Nolte, but without the hair or charisma. There's a definite gulf between what I think I'm putting out into the world and what I actually am. If I was a raccoon, or even a dog looking for a home, I'd have died of starvation by now.

But lucky for me, I've got money. I decide to take a walk to the coffee shop near my office for a cookie and coffee, and I pay for it with two toonies. The clerk takes them and holds one in each hand.

"This one feels heavier," she says, holding up her left hand.

I ask for the coins back, to see for myself. The smallest unit of weight I'm able to think in terms of is the Quarter Pounder™. When considering how much my father's toy poodle weighs, I think "twenty Quarter Pounders" and from there convert into imperial units.

"I can't tell the difference," I say. "Perhaps you have a hidden talent."

She smiles. Everyone has a hidden talent for something. The lucky ones discover theirs before it's too late. Would it be more sad or less sad to go through life never discovering you can fly, or discovering it only a minute before dying? I guess it would really allow for a beautiful death—an old man flying out the window after a long life.

I take my coffee, sip it, and wonder how many coffees I've left to go.

THURSDAY.

I'm with Helen and Katie, auditioning a story I've written for my radio show. In the middle of my reading, Marie-Claude enters the room and sends them outside to play.

"What wrong with you?" she asks. "Why are you reading my children a story about death?"

"It's existential," I say. "Plus, they asked me to read it."

"My nine- and seven-year-old said, 'Please, Uncle Jonny, favour us with a story about death'? Are you insane?"

"As their godfather, I have a responsibility to offer lessons in spiritual hygiene."

"You? Hygiene? Helen says you told her that when you were her age you only bathed once a week."

"I wanted her to know that everyone is different," I

say. "That's why there are career aptitude tests. The kids who bathe every day will be more inclined towards work in the public sector—making pastries and giving tours of model homes; while the once-a-week kids might be more comfortable hoboing, bohoing, or radio show–hosting. And in this way, we maintain a balance."

Marie-Claude does not buy my version of a just society, and throws me out of her house.

SEIZING THE DAY

———

There once was a man named Chalchas the Greek. When he was only a young lad, Chalchas learned that he would one day die.

"It happens to all of us," his father said. "It's just the way things go."

The boy was surprised by the news. Sure, his father would die. Yes, his mother and even his brothers and sister would die. His grandfather had already died, as had the heroes he learned about at school. This all made sense to him. But that he, Chalchas the Greek, would die? No, there had to be a glitch in there somewhere.

Though it didn't make sense to his heart, he knew it to be true intellectually, and so each morning Chalchas awoke and thought, "Today could be the day I die."

On some days, he was struck with the thought several hundred times. It became impossible to focus on anything else. Back then, there were no psychiatrists or therapists, so Chalchas went to see an oracle.

The old oracle lived in the forest, on the outskirts of town. It was a full day's journey there, and when Chalchas found him, he was sitting in the shade of a large tree, staring up at the sky with wide-open eyes. Chalchas wasted no time in getting to the point.

"I want to know when I'll die," he said.

Chalchas figured that if he could just know how much time he had left, he could relax. A man only died once, but the way he was worrying, it felt like he was going through the motions of dying every day.

After a few attempts at dissuading him, the oracle acquiesced, revealing to Chalchas the precise day upon which his death would arrive. It was a pretty far-off day, though perhaps not as far off as Chalchas would have liked. If he was honest with himself, he was in fact hoping the oracle would consult his great book of death and, flipping back and forth between pages, finally utter, "That's odd. I have no listing here for Chalchas the Greek. It would seem you do not die. How weird is that?"

And so the days passed and the day of Chalchas's death grew nearer just as the day of all of our deaths draws nearer. Except Chalchas was able to count down to his. Each morning he would awake and think, "2764 to go. 1873. 922."

As the days dwindled, what once felt like a vast number of days—an ocean—slowly became a paltry year. And then that paltry year became a few skeletal months, and then, what felt like very suddenly, those months turned into weeks and when they did, Chalchas took to himself. He wanted to be alone in his final days to really cherish each second without distraction.

"I've only a few days to go," he'd say in a sweat.

And then the day arrived. By now Chalchas was an old man, but mostly he felt okay, no major pains or issues. So when he awoke he looked around, took a few breaths, waited, and then, realizing he was still alive, Chalchas the Greek began to laugh.

"Ha ha," he chortled. "Hee hee."

So great was his merriment over having fooled the fates that Chalchas threw his arms up in the air and executed a jig.

"Hardee har. Hoo hoo ha hee hee hee. How absurd to have worried!" he exclaimed through his laughter. "What do oracles know?" Oracle! The very word was ridiculous and enough to make him twice as giggly.

No longer able to contain himself, Chalchas fell

to the ground and pounded the earth with all his might. He laughed and laughed and punched and punched until his fists failed to clench, his lungs ceased to inflate, his throat could produce no sound, and his mind became free of all things, even thoughts of his own death.

Atonement

(48 weeks)

WEDNESDAY.

The evening finds me squatting in front of a gumball machine, cursing. In want of one more treat before beginning the Yom Kippur fast, I've inserted a quarter and nothing's happened. As much as I assure myself that my outrage is not about the money but about the broken social compact, I still cannot help feeling that bear-hugging a gumball machine on my knees might actually be the first thing I've discovered in quite some time to truly be beneath my dignity.

Who would be the perfect person to walk by at this moment? An old schoolteacher who never thought I'd amount to much? An ex-girlfriend's father who could never stand my guts?

When I was a kid, my parents had a needlepoint of Moses. In it, he's giving the commandments to the children of Israel. Despite many important moments in Moses's life, that one is probably the signature one. I can't help thinking that wrestling this gumball machine might be mine.

And as I continue to work, my finger up the gum hole, I cannot help imagining what this would look like as a needlepoint.

THURSDAY, 2:00 A.M.

I lie awake, hungry and thinking about God. I wonder: Am I a good enough person to get into Heaven? How does it all get tallied up anyway? Is my love of processed meat counterbalanced by the fastidious recycling of my scotch bottles? In gas stations and convenience stores, I take a penny more often than I leave a penny, but I am a more than generous tipper—even in buffet-type situations.

3:45 A.M.

For all we know about the workings of the universe, entry into Heaven might depend solely on shoe size. Nines go to hell and elevens go to Heaven, where their snowshoe-like feet are able to tromp atop clouds without falling through.

I am reminded of Grushenka in *The Brothers Karamazov*, who thinks she'll be saved because she once gave a peasant an onion. All it takes is a single pure deed, she believes. I wish I had her confidence.

4:30 A.M.

I've always held on to the irrational hope that in my final days I might suddenly transform into one of those Zorba-the-Greek kind of guys. I wonder if you can spend your whole life never coming ten thousand miles within seizing the day and then finally, at the last minute, turn it all around and redeem everything. In my final hours, I want to wander into the backyard in my deathbed bathrobe and, despite everything left undone—the European vacations, the Ski-Doo rides over the tundra—spread out my arms and do one of those life-embracing Zorba dances.

"Look at the big dancing phony," God will probably say, watching in Heaven. "It's going to take more than showmanship to get into paradise on my watch."

4:45 A.M.

Fasting does funny things to a man's faith. An inner dialogue takes place in which you argue for and against the existence of God based solely on how in the mood you are for a muffin and coffee.

What if Henry Heimlich Were Choking?
(47 weeks)

SUNDAY.

I'm over at Tucker's. He's just gotten a sandwich press and has been spending the day inventing new sandwiches. He's working on a dessert sandwich called the Lew Wasserman Special. It's made of Rice Krispies, marshmallows, cocoa, and candy sprinkles.

"Ever notice how people keep candy sprinkles in their spice rack?" Tucker asks, applying his body weight to the press. "Since when are candy sprinkles a spice?"

"Since the time brave European explorers set out along trade routes in search of new ways to decorate their cupcakes."

"It's a mockery of the whole concept of spice!"

"Speaking of spice," I say, "what do you think your Spice Girl name would be? Angry Spice?"

"I don't have a Spice Girl name. I have a fighting name: The Gefilte Fist. What's your Spice Girl name?"

"Paprika."

Gefilte and paprika go well together, just like Tucker and me and, I'm hoping, marshmallows and sandwich bread.

MONDAY.

With flu season upon us, so as not to be expected to shake hands or turn doorknobs, I've taken to walking the halls of my office with a cup of coffee in each hand. As a result, I am keeping twice as caffeinated. And twice as sweaty and shaky. By the end of the day, my clothes are drenched in spilled coffee and perspiration.

I'm not the only one at work worried about germs. All day long, we rub antibacterial soap into our hands. It has the effect of making us look like the evil, scheming characters in a Renaissance drama. If only people could be so obvious about their secret schemes! It would make buying a used car easier, though dating impossible.

TUESDAY.

I'm sitting in my doctor's waiting room waiting to get a flu shot. Presented with the choice of reading an issue of *Medical Economics* or doing a newspaper crossword puzzle,

I pick up the crossword. Unfortunately, I seem to have lost my pen, and so I do the puzzle in my head. I'm normally terrible at crosswords, but for some reason, today I'm on fire, getting every single answer and holding it all in my mind. What's the point of solving a crossword puzzle that no one can see? I'm sure it has something to do with character or integrity, but at the moment I'd settle for being able to impress the receptionist.

FRIDAY.

Free from the worry of contagion, I meet my parents for dinner at their favourite restaurant. As I slide into the booth, I am overcome with a spirit of playfulness. It's a feeling I'm touched by only three or four times every ten years, so I decide to indulge it. I do so by encouraging my father to order a plate of the fattiest cut of smoked meat.

"I've been practising the Heimlich technique," I tell him. "My power and precision are fierce enough to send a choking man's gristle twelve feet across the room and land it in a martini glass."

"Choking isn't a joke," my mother says, "and neither is eating red meat. I've already ordered fish and chicken for the table."

Over dinner we speak of the blandness of the fish and the dryness of the chicken and, intermittently, my mother interrupts the conversation to return our water because

a) the ice looks dirty, or b) the water tastes like "bathroom sink" water.

Ten minutes into the meal, and I've lost my spirit of playfulness. I consider sinking under the table, and re-emerging only after my family has left and a new family has replaced them. Maybe in time, this new family will become my family.

"This fish is too fishy-tasting," my father says, and we all nod our heads in agreement.

"I am. I am. I am."
(46 weeks)

SUNDAY.

On the news, I watch the outrage caused by a potential ban on poutine at a local ice-skating arena. The reporter explains to the woefully ignorant that poutine is a combination of fries, gravy, and cheese curds, but to see it as only that is to miss the magic, to forget that atoms form molecules possessing entirely new properties. I mean, if the sun is not mere hydrogen and helium but, as William Blake saw it, innumerable angels singing "holy, holy, holy," then poutine is at the very least an obese, sticky-faced cherub having a heart attack.

I watch amazed by the power poutine has to rally a community.

"It goes against our right to be fat," says an indignant local politician. I am not a very political man, but I am moved by his words.

MONDAY.

In the bathroom at work, I place my hands under the faucet. Water is supposed to start automatically, but nothing happens. I switch to another sink and still, nothing. After a lot of waving my arms around, I turn on the taps myself, wash my hands, and go over to the dryer. Nothing. It's like I'm a hologram. The irrational fear that I don't exist is a recurring theme in my life, and it's as if everything I do is in order to prove to myself that I am actually here. But despite my best efforts, I feel as though the automatic hand dryer in my office bathroom understands me better than anyone else.

"You're not really here," it says to me. "You may think you are, but you aren't."

On the way back to my desk, I hum to myself, "I am. I am. I am."

THURSDAY.

I'm looking after Boosh for my father. We're sitting on the couch watching a video when Tony calls.

"What's up?" he asks.

I tell him I'm eating popcorn, drinking wine, and watching a movie with Boosh.

"Sorry to interrupt your date," he says.

"What are you talking about?" I say, peeved. "We're not on a date."

"What movie are you watching?"

"*All About Steve*," I say. "With Sandra Bullock."

"So you're watching a romantic comedy that I assume you paid for, and drinking wine. Dude, you're on a date with a dog."

I hang up the phone, un-dim the lights, and put the cork back in the bottle, my date ruined.

FRIDAY.

Walking back to my office after lunch, I lose my thought. I am left with no trace whatsoever of the thought's content, but I do have the overall *feeling* that the thought has left behind: a certain *looking forward-ness*. Despite having forgotten what I am actually looking forward *to*, knowing that there's something out there that I'd previously assessed to be *worth* looking forward to is a nice enough feeling. After a few seconds, though, I realize that what I was looking forward to was the piece of uneaten Melba toast from yesterday's lunch that I'd left in my desk drawer.

Back at my office, the sadness I feel for having looked forward to the Melba toast overwhelms the happiness I feel while eating the Melba toast. Overall, I am left feeling pretty even.

Friends Who Do Not Kill You
Make You Stronger
(45 weeks)

SUNDAY.

Gregor comes over for breakfast. A business breakfast. He instructs me to save the bill for the groceries so that I can expense it.

"This is warm bread," he says. "You lack the stick-to-itness to make toast. And even the way you cut it is wrong. Toast has to be cut diagonally. Not vertically. This is an abomination."

"If manners are going out the window, then I'll say this: Quit double-fisting the strawberries. I might want to have one myself."

"How dare you!" he yells. "You're the double-fister! Remember that time I ran into you on the street and you were eating from a bag of Cheezies with your left hand and a bag of Fritos with your right? Coming down the street it looked like you were wearing mittens."

"I was wearing mittens."

"Even worse! What grown man wears mittens?"

"Why can't we just enjoy breakfast," I say. "Why do you always have to focus on what's wrong with everything?"

"It's a talent and a curse," Gregor says sombrely. "I guess I'm just more sensitive than most."

"Did you know that after eighteen years locked in the darkness, Kaspar Hauser's eyes were so sensitive to light he could see stars in the daytime?"

"Maybe to his friends it seemed like an ability to see blemishes in a perfectly bright sunshiny day."

"Okay," I say. "But to even be able to see stars you have to start by looking up and taking in the glory of the firmament once in a while."

In a dramatic flourish, I lean my head back and stretch out my arms as though embracing the world, flaws and all. In so doing, I knock a pot of coffee off the table. It shatters, sending coffee and glass in all directions.

I rise from the table.

"Don't bother getting up to help with the mess," I say.

"What mess?" he asks, continuing to eat his warm bread.

THURSDAY.

Tucker and I are supposed to go out for steak tonight. We frequent this place where the average customer age is eighty-five. Going there makes us feel young and virile. But an hour before we're set to go, he calls up.

"I don't feel steaky," he says.

I ask him why and he explains how he misplayed his whole day of eating and now he just isn't ready.

"I was working on my film treatment at the café this afternoon," he says, "and I spilled coffee all over it. But the amazing thing was that the coffee stain perfectly high-lighted the opening two paragraphs, and I realized, looking at them like that, that they needed to be completely rewritten. All of this because of the spill! I began to wonder if God had finally taken notice of me. I tested this theory by seeing if the girl sitting beside me would talk to me. She would not, and so to cheer myself, I ordered a half-pound Angus burger with fries."

Unfortunately there's no Viagra for steak. I put the phone down and go make myself a sandwich. If God is taking notice of me, there will be Dijon left in the pantry.

FRIDAY.

Howard is going away for the weekend and I've agreed to watch his pugs, Desmond and Bruce. He shows up at my apartment with, among other things, two dog beds, three vinyl pork chops, chicken-flavoured toothpaste, and a canvas chew bone upon which are inscribed the words "Bite me."

"Is all this necessary?" I ask. "A two-pound bag of heart-shaped dog treats? How many treat-worthy deeds can two dogs accomplish over the course of a single weekend?"

"I like to lavish my boys with positive reinforcement," he says. "Finish all the food in your bowl: that's a treat. Go to the bathroom: that's a treat."

"Eat all your treats: that's a treat."

"Look," Howard says. "They can tell we're talking about them!"

I look down. A string of drool hangs from Desmond's lip while Bruce scratches an ear with his hind leg.

"The weight of their stoic hearkening fills the room like a dense fog."

"They're enlightened," Howard says defensively. "Pugs were bred by Tibetan monks. Do you know what for? Not sheep herding or sled pulling, but for companionship."

Before leaving, Howard tells me that Desmond and Bruce will prove to be the best friends I've ever had. Sadly, I fear his words may actually prove correct.

Guys' Night Out

(44 weeks)

SATURDAY.

My father doesn't get out much, but when he does, he enjoys himself. The man is certainly capable of joy. It's just that his happiness makes my mother uncomfortable. Whenever he starts to come out of his shell, she likes to cram him right back in there. So disco dancing at weddings, eating dessert with too much gusto—even drumming on the kitchen table to a radio jingle—all rub my mother the wrong way. If my father even laughs too loudly, my mother tells him he's getting "punchy." That usually quiets him down.

So the first order of business is getting him out of the house.

After all, it is his birthday.

3:45 P.M.

"Come over," I say to him over the phone. "We'll go out and celebrate a little. Just me and you."

Whenever I get together with my father, I can't help seeing it as a chance to nurse him back to health. Really, all we're doing is heading downtown for a bite to eat, but my father is wonderfully easy to please. One time, about ten years ago, we took a walk to the old part of the city and he still talks about it to this day.

"Remember how hot it was?" my father asks me every few months. "Remember how we had to stop in at that convenience store and each of us got a soda? You got a Coke, and so did I. We drank them straight from the can— no straw, no cup. Just like that. Like construction workers. Like street hustlers!"

4:00 P.M.

When he gets to my apartment, I offer to take over the driving. He gets into the passenger seat, and right off the bat he says, "Being chauffeured makes me feel like I'm on vacation." When he's with my mother, my father does all the driving while my mother sits shotgun, elbows bent, pointing her house keys towards the front-door lock from forty miles away.

"What do you want to do?" I ask.

He waves a hand and tells me he doesn't need pampering.

Pampering! Since the mid-eighties, the man has been using the same ninety-nine-cent VHS tape to record and re-record the same documentaries about Nazi hunting. He keeps his cufflinks in a washed-out yogurt container on his dresser. When I was growing up, any time a roll of toilet paper accidentally fell in the toilet, my mother would set it to dry on the basin and forbid me from using it, referring to it as "your father's toilet paper." He has a meatball-shaped wallet made of vinyl, fat with expired coupons. When he sits down he looks like a wobbling Weeble.

4:30 P.M.

The first thing I want to do is find us a fancy bar. My father enjoys a drink, and at home, he usually can't enjoy one properly. Unfortunately traffic is bad, and parking is even worse, so by the time we find a spot, my father is ready for supper.

After debating the meaning of various contradictory parking signs with the fervour of Talmud scholars, my father looks around.

"The area looks seedy," he says.

We check and recheck the car doors and windows, and finally, we're on our way.

4:45 P.M.

As we walk along, my father comments on everything he sees, his index fingers pointing every which way as though he's on a tour bus through Paris or he's a character in a Menudo video going to a shopping mall for the first time. A panhandler! A boy with a hoop through his lip like a witch doctor! An unsavoury-looking character who might be a pickpocket!

4:50 P.M.

We find a Middle Eastern restaurant which, to be honest, is more of a cafeteria. We each order a big plate of chicken and rice, and as we eat, we drink a beer each. Beer helps my father relax. Rather than eating hunched over as though planning a prison break, he reclines and looks around. At home, he finishes a great many of his meals with the plate yanked away in mid-bite, forced to finish his corn on the cob stooped over the sink.

"What kind of rice is this?" he asks.

"White," I say.

"I'll have to ask your mother to buy some."

5:25 P.M.

Finished eating, we head back to the car. There are no tickets on the windshield, and the *Chicago's Greatest Hits* audio cassette still sits on the dashboard, unstolen. The afternoon has been a success.

7:10 P.M.

I call the house later to make sure my father has made it back okay, and my mother answers. She says he's downstairs eating peanuts at the kitchen table.

"He had such a fabulous time with you today," she says a little suspiciously. "He can't stop talking about it."

I ask her if he enjoyed the meal we had, and she tells me not to feed my father garbage. Beer keeps him up all night, and he has to watch his cholesterol.

"When's the last time you had yours checked?" she asks.

I really can't recall. My mother is always reminding me how her brother had a heart attack when he was around my age.

After I put down the phone, I stop to imagine, as I find myself doing lately, several times a day, what my heart attack would look like. It would be an undignified, pulling-down-the-drapes, cheeks-bulging-with-veal sort of thing. It would be the kind of heart attack that friends would laughingly imitate in the kitchen during my shiva, my mother shushing them from the other room.

bed

(43 weeks)

SUNDAY.

I'm lying in bed watching old episodes of *Deadwood* on my laptop. The laptop is resting on my chest in what I like to call "the deathbed style." By watching the movie in this manner, I have come to see how it is not about the size of the screen in one's "home entertainment unit," but about how close you can get the screen to your face. Pressed against your nose, fourteen inches is just like IMAX, but the problem inherent to this method is that it is only good for one. Also, it is stupid-looking. Really stupid-looking.

The characters on *Deadwood* are constantly drinking whisky or taking dope. If I lived in Deadwood, I'd be in a continual state of anxiety, always trembling, terrified I was about to be shot in the ass or worse. I wouldn't even look at people, for fear of inciting their wrath. I'd slither around on the ground between people's legs, apologizing and avoiding eye contact. *Thank God I don't live in Deadwood*, I think while pouring Skittles into my mouth.

THURSDAY.

I'm over for dinner at Marie-Claude's and while she's cooking, I make conversation with Katie.

"Ever notice how the word 'bed' looks like a bed?" I ask.

"Not 'pillow,' though," she says.

"And what's up with pimentos?" I ask, picking up an olive from the plate on the coffee table. "What are they anyway?"

"They're red," she says, keeping up her end of the conversation. "Where do you think pimento trees grow?"

"Inside olive trees."

"Stop filling my daughter's head with garbage," Marie-Claude says, walking into the living room and putting down a tray of cheese and crackers. "And do me a favour and shave your beard already. It's unsanitary."

I'd lately begun growing it back. Running my hand across my cheek in a way I hope looks thoughtful, I say, "People tell me it makes me look intellectual. And more youthful."

"It makes you look like a hostage," Marie-Claude says, leaving the room.

"Mama's only joking," I say to Katie. Katie takes off her shoes and asks if she can rub her bare feet in my beard.

Marie-Claude re-enters the room to find her daughter doing the moonwalk on my cheek.

"Katie," Marie-Claude says, "go wash your feet."

FRIDAY.

At work, I confide to David, a fellow radio producer, that I've lately been feeling an overwhelming urge to lie down on the sidewalk on my walk to work.

"I'm overcome by this feeling that I can't go on," I say.

David tells me to be careful not to get arrested for vagrancy.

"On days when I feel especially frustrated," he says, "I always make sure to give myself a nice close shave before leaving the house. That way, if I start yelling in the street, people will be less inclined to see me as a garden-variety street lunatic, and more like a man wheeling and dealing into his Bluetooth."

I decide that shave again I must. Sometimes it's worth making the effort of personal hygiene, if only to afford yourself the freedom of antisocial pleasures.

The Great Gazoo

(42 weeks)

SUNDAY.

I stare at myself in the mirror, shaving cream covering my face.

Mid-shave is a good look for me. A face full of lather really brings out my eyes. I wish this could be some kind of style—something to leave the house in.

I imagine myself at Tony and Natalie's wedding, toasting the bride and groom in a three-piece suit—a face brushed white, erasing all blemishes. I could always become a clown, but when I'd take a cream pie across the face, instead of making the audience laugh, I'd make them gasp at my sudden, horrifying beauty.

THURSDAY.

I'm meeting Tony for coffee. When I sit down, I find him drinking from a coffee cup the size of a fire hydrant.

"The other day I watched a Steve McQueen movie from the seventies," I say. "Do you have any idea how small coffees were back then? The way things are evolving, in a couple more generations, we'll be ordering coffees using mattress sizes. 'One queen-sized soy latte to go.'"

"I've always hoped that one day in the future I could walk into a coffee shop and have the counterman ask, 'With or without Sea-Monkeys?' It would be like bubble tea, but with bubbles that do tricks."

After a silent stretch spent staring out the window at the falling rain, Tony asks, "If you could eat only one or the other for the rest of your life, which would you choose: Baby Aspirins or Flintstone Vitamins?"

"Based solely on taste or curative properties?"

"Just taste," he says.

"Flintstones," I say. "The Great Gazoo in particular. Did you know he was exiled to Earth for inventing a machine that could destroy the universe with the push of a button? When I was a kid, I used to think about that a lot."

"When I was a kid," says Tony, "I thought about brontosaurus ribs a lot."

FRIDAY.

Still thinking about the food of my youth, I'm struck by the realization that I no longer have friends who make Jell-O shooters. I don't even have friends of friends who make Jell-O shooters. Let me be clear: I never actually liked Jell-O shooters, but I guess I just assumed they'd always be around. And now their memory has become more potent than what they were. Which was disgusting.

Even so tiny a loss has the power to still feel like a loss. Forty slowly descends like a mid-November frost.

LOSS OF MEMORY

There was once a man who felt his losses more acutely than others. Lost watches. Umbrellas. A money clip. He just couldn't let go. The passage of time didn't help, either. He still dreamt of childhood toys he hadn't seen in years.

And of course there was the loss of women, some of whom he still woke up aching for. He'd study their remnants alone at night—slips of paper bearing old phone numbers. Photographs. A mitten. In bed he would stare at the ceiling, trying to seize on the exact feeling of a particular woman's head on his chest. Its weight, the smell of her hair.

And yet oddly, the majority of these recollections were almost perfectly wrong. His memory turned redheads into brunettes, French women into Spaniards. Awful women into saints.

One day while waiting for his bath to fill—he

lived in a building with ancient plumbing and it often took hours—the man went out to buy a magazine to read while bathing, and on the street he ran into one of those ex-girlfriends of his. She was staring into the window of a candy store, and when he approached her there was not a shred of recognition in her eyes. He told her his name, repeated it, pointed at his face, and still, it was like staring into an abyss. He worried this might be some game she was playing. A hurtful game.

As he turned to leave, the woman touched his shoulder and explained that, about two months earlier, she'd been in an accident and had lost many of her memories. Some she kept. Small ones. The colour of old blankets. A mole on a kindergarten teacher's face. But most of the big ones had been wiped out.

"You might have been a big one," she said and smiled.

It was in seeing the woman smile that the man immediately realized this was not his ex-girlfriend at all. His ex-girlfriend did not have a gap between her front teeth. His ex-girlfriend in fact looked nothing like this woman.

"If you're not too busy," the woman continued, "I'd love to hear about us. The things we did. What I was like back then. What we were like together."

She suggested a nearby café, and the man, not sure what to do, began to stammer and hesitate.

"Please," she said. "I've been so lonely without my memories."

And so with nothing else to do besides wait for his bath to fill, the man acquiesced. *To lose a fountain pen is one thing*, he thought. *But to lose one's entire self!* It was clear this woman needed him.

Seated at a table in the rear of the café, he searched for where to start.

"Well," he said, "we went out for hamburgers quite a bit. Milkshakes, too, and you always insisted on paying. It was your thing. Our thing."

"I don't eat many hamburgers these days," the woman said with amusement. "I'm mostly vegetarian."

"And we always sat on the same side of the booth," he said.

The woman listened to him recount her past, taking it all in, sometimes with closed eyes as though soaking up sunshine and other times shaking her head with disbelief. Occasionally, she would throw her head back and laugh.

"When you drank soda," he said, "you held the can backwards, like a cute little monkey."

She tried it out with her mug and felt the coffee dribble down her chin.

"I still do that sometimes," she said uncertainly.

"You had this way of rubbing my head furiously when I'd bang it," he said. "I banged it often."

Some of the things he tried to remind her of sounded familiar, and made her feel like she was entering a warm, carpeted room; but other times, the things he spoke of seemed so alien that they made her feel like she was hopping out of a cake onto a cold, dark stage.

"One time," he said, "we were trying to get out of the rain and we mistakenly ran into an S and M bar. There was a TV in the back and we watched an old episode of *Frasier*."

He was painting a portrait made from the bits of memory he'd stored from all the women he'd ever loved. Brandy's fondness for American sitcoms. Nancy's joie de vivre. Kathy's impenetrable melancholy. Meaghan's enthusiasm for the smell of toast. Or was it socks from the dryer?

"You liked raisins and you liked chocolate," he said. "But you did not like chocolate-covered raisins. You enjoyed it when I sat on the lid of the toilet and talked to you while you showered."

The more he painted, the more he experienced the sensation of falling in love. With something. Or someone. Possibly her. It seemed the woman was feeling something, too.

She was in fact feeling something indeed. For as the man spoke, as he leaned towards her, closer and closer, the smell of his coffee breath was slowly turning her stomach. And with the smell crept spiders of memory. His morning breath. The way he would speak so close to her that she'd have to wipe spittle from her glasses.

"So much is coming back to me," she began.

Yes, the woman thought. *I'm certain this must be why we broke up. Those noises he makes while drinking. The way he doesn't let me get in a word edgewise.*

"You'd made me promise," he said, "that if you were ever kidnapped or locked away somewhere, that I would never give up, never rest until you were free."

The man leaned forward and looked at her with great intensity, and as his bathroom flooded with bathwater and his downstairs neighbour pounded on his apartment door with increasing fury, he knew he was succeeding in making her remember.

The Tears You Cry in Dreams
(41 weeks)

SUNDAY.

After helping my parents clean their garage, I decide to sleep over. It was a long night spent convincing my father how certain things were better off being thrown out, like a box of microfiches, considering he doesn't even own a microfiche projector.

"Once the internet fizzles, they could come back," he said. "Look at vinyl."

In the middle of the night, I'm awakened by a dream in which my lap is on fire. Some back story:

When I was a child our family used to eat at a restaurant called Pumpernick's, a kosher-style tiki bar–restaurant where the husbands made sport of driving their wives as close to the front door as possible. This often involved getting right up on the curb, almost killing anyone foolish enough to lolly-gag after a meal.

When dining there, my sister and I usually shared a hamburger, but my dream was to one day have the flaming Pu-Pu platter, a dish of chicken, onion rings, wontons, and God-knows-what, all brought to the table ablaze. The diner had to blow it out like a plate full of birthday candles, or a stray Molotov cocktail. To a ten-year-old, a Pu-Pu platter turned dining into an act of heroism.

In the dream, even though it closed down years ago, I am back at Pumpernick's. It is late at night and when I walk in, the cashier tells me they're closed.

"I've come a long way," I say. "Just one quick Pu-Pu?"

She gives in and tells me I can have one. To go.

The flaming tray is brought out, I pay the bill, and walk out into the night to catch a bus back home. As I ride through the night, the fiery plate jostles to and fro on my lap. I am nervous and want to tell the driver to slow down, but then it is too late: my lap is on fire.

I awake to find Boosh, curled up, asleep on my groin.

I am becoming more and more like my father. Yearnful for things that no longer exist. But in spite of this, my father and I are happy men—happy that, at the very least, we are not on fire.

It's already morning, but I don't want to disturb Boosh, so I lie still, staring at the ceiling and trying to decide what to do with the day.

MONDAY.

It appears that someone has taken a candy out of the office candy dish, removed its wrapper, sucked it, and put it back in the bowl where it now sits stuck to the bottom, red, wet, and gleaming. Someone who is capable of something like that is capable of anything. There is a sociopath among us. I make a mental note to stop using the communal office dishrag and start keeping my uneaten Melba toast in a locked desk drawer.

FRIDAY.

No one has removed the candy from the candy bowl.

In my teens, when I kept notebooks filled with poetry, the lone candy, tasted but not chosen, might have been the kind of thing that could've made me cry. Back then, pretty much anything did—an old man eating by himself in a restaurant. Songs by Carole King. Commercials for long distance calls. And then one day the crying stopped. Sitting at my desk, it strikes me: I haven't cried in close to twenty years.

When the executive producer of my show, Carolyn, stops by, I share this with her.

"The closest I come is sometimes I dream I'm crying," I say.

She tells me that her friend had the same problem and her therapist told her that the only tears that are real are the tears you cry in dreams.

Too bad the same can't be said of the Pu-Pu platters you eat.

Two Yarmulkes

(40 weeks)

SUNDAY.

I'm dog-sitting Boosh at my apartment, and when I arrive home I find the kitchen garbage scattered all across the living room. The dog is out of control. In the middle of the night, she awakens me with lavish licks to my shaved head like she's working away at a Tootsie Pop. What's even more unsettling is that the sensation is disturbingly tender and maternal.

TUESDAY.

Before heading out to the store, I make sure to put on some thermal underwear. As I've gotten older, long johns have become more and more important. When I was a child, my father warned against them.

"You get used to long underwear," he said, "and then you can't take them off. July rolls around and you've still got them on under a pair of jean shorts. And then by the winter, you need two pairs—and the winter after that, three!"

For my father, long johns are much the same as heroin.

FRIDAY.

The laces on my shoes keep snapping. It feels like I've been going through about half a dozen a month. Every time I tie them, I think: "They can break right now. Or even now." It fills me with *Weltschmerz*, and really, who wants to start the day with *Weltschmerz*?

I'm probably pulling too hard, though maybe I've somehow been endowed with supernatural strength. Maybe the moth I shooed out of my sports jacket last month was radioactive. Perhaps the ripping of my shoelaces is the first manifestation of my superpower—a superpower for wearing away at fabric.

When I stop by Tucker's for a beer, I share this thought with him.

"Your only superpower is for wearing away at people's patience," he says.

As I'm leaving his apartment and putting on my shoes, again, my shoelace rips.

"You see?" I say, vindicated.

Tucker disappears into his apartment and returns with a bag. A shoelace bag.

Tucker is a man who doesn't have an ice tray, a doorbell, or even a functioning smoke detector—but a shoelace bag he has.

He pulls out a pair of thick laces the length of skipping ropes.

"These won't break," he says. "They're for hockey skates."

I lace them through my shoes and still have enough left over to crisscross up my calf like a Roman sandal. As I walk home, I try to convince myself that I am a gladiator. For the first time in a while, I actually feel less anxious about my footwear.

I.B. Singer writes of a Hassid who is so religious, he wears two yarmulkes—one on the front of his head and one on the back, just in case. Whereas the Hassid is anxiously devoted to his religion, I am religiously devoted to my anxiety. And to long johns. I'm sure the overzealous Hassid and I both appear ludicrous in the eyes of God, but at least I am not cold.

Knights of the Roundtable
(39 weeks)

SATURDAY, 1:15 P.M.

As a change in the regular format of the show, Mira and I set up a line for people to call in with their personal problems, and today we've convened a roundtable of advice-givers: my father, goddaughter Helen, and Howard.

"It's always been a dream of mine to be part of a round-table," Howard says, sitting down at the studio microphone, "but I somehow always imagined there'd be a cheese platter involved."

2:35 P.M.

We listen to Stephanie from Montreal's phone message. She's a self-described nerd looking to meet a boy nerd.

"How can I help her?" my father asks, sounding genuinely stumped. "I know nothing of nerds."

"Me neither," Howard says.

"How can you say that?" I ask Howard. "You are a nerd. You collect *Star Wars* dolls, for crying out loud."

"They're from *Star Trek*," he says. "And they're collector's figurines."

"I think that except for in the movies, there's really no such thing as a nerd," says Helen.

"Just a lot of lonely people looking for someone to hold on to," says Howard.

"And our next caller," I say, leaning into the microphone.

3:10 P.M.

Laurie from Vancouver wants to know what can be done about people peeing in pools.

"More poolside bathrooms," Helen says.

"Or what about dividing the pool," Howard says. "Instead of a shallow end and a deep end, you have a peeing section and a non-peeing section."

"That's disgusting," my father says.

3:45 P.M.

Rebecca from London, Ontario, wants to know what to do about the tantalizing smell of cooking wafting through the vent from her neighbour's apartment. It's making her hungry all the time.

"I try to fend off the smell by making bread and cookies," she says. "Since this whole thing started, I've gained ten pounds."

"Rebecca, don't try to combat good smells with good smells," Howard says. "Combat good smells with bad smells. Stop bathing, don't flush, and sprinkle patchouli oil liberally around the apartment."

"That's disgusting," Helen says.

4:00 P.M.

Steve from Ottawa has just broken up with his very first girlfriend.

"How do you get over a first love?" he asks.

"You never do," Howard says. "It just stays with you and becomes a part of who you are."

I ask my father if he still remembers his first love.

"Of course I do," he says. "I was still in high school. It was really nice."

But when I ask him for details, like what her name was, he starts to blush and get uncomfortable.

Even though it's over fifty years ago, he's still afraid to get in trouble with my mother.

4:40 P.M.

After the last message the roundtable is adjourned.

"We did some really good work," my father says.

"Maybe next time we can do it on a weekday," Helen says, "so I can get out of school."

"And maybe next time," Howard says, "we can get a cheese platter."

Unpredictable

(38 weeks)

MONDAY.

I put down the phone, sweating and breathing hard.

"Who were you arguing with?" Marie-Claude asks. She's over at my place, visiting with Helen and Katie.

"My dad—and we weren't arguing. I was trying to explain that it's impossible for him to have gotten an email 'from the internet.'"

I look over and see that Helen and Katie are reading a book of Garfield comics.

"I feel bad for Jon," Helen says.

"Why?" I ask. "He has a pretty sweet deal. A dog. A cat. A coffee mug, as well as a counter upon which he can place his coffee mug."

"But when was the last time he had a meal?" she asks. "Garfield's always eating all his food. It doesn't make sense that he hasn't died of starvation yet."

I want to explain to Helen and Katie that it's not just comics that don't make sense, that life doesn't make sense either, but I'm not sure how to put it, so instead I tell them that Jon probably eats his meals between the panels and that, in fact, most of life occurs between the panels.

We should probably acknowledge life's nonsensical nature more often, though. I'm not saying it should be brought up a hundred times a day, but maybe once in a while—to keep things in perspective. Like when the president finishes a speech, he could look into the TV camera and say, "But still, we really don't know anything at all. Life is unknowable, and one day we'll all die without ever having made much sense out of it. It's weird."

Saying stuff like that should replace "Good night" and "God bless."

WEDNESDAY.

I'm downtown at a remaindered bookstore, browsing through fad diet cookbooks from the nineties, when I come across a book called *The Amazing Kreskin's Future with the Stars*, published in 2001. The famed mentalist sent out letters to celebrities asking for their predictions about the future and then turned their responses into a book— even including the letters from celebrities who wrote back that they weren't interested in participating. I suppose if you're going to place "The Amazing" in front of your name, you've got to have a certain amount of chutzpah.

Flipping through the book, I see that Ed McMahon envisioned a world where television would one day be projected onto the clouds, and that Roseanne Barr prophesied she would be the greatest television talk-show host of all time.

Who'd have thought cloud TV would prove a more sane prediction?

I grab an unauthorized biography of Angela Lansbury and leave.

SATURDAY.

"Did you know that Angela Lansbury's son was in the Manson gang?" I ask Tony over the phone. "Or that she played Laurence Harvey's mother in *The Manchurian Candidate* even though she was only three years older than him?"

"I'm not a fan of celebrity bios," he says, "but I especially hate those ones from rock stars where they conclude the book with stuff like, 'I'd flush all the cocaine and ménages à trois down the toilet for the love of one good woman.' What a crock."

"But you're a one-woman man," I say. "You wouldn't trade Natalie for a Natalie-sized statue of Natalie made of cocaine."

"It's just easy for the guitarist from Aerosmith to sing the praises of settling down when he's got twenty-eight thousand one-night stands under his belt."

Tony considers his own words for a moment.

"I should tweet that," he says.

"Could you imagine our grandfathers tweeting?"

"From the age of eight my grandfather worked nineteen hours a day milking goats and digging wells," Tony says. "He'd never have had time for social media."

I think about my dad emailing up a storm. Then I consider *his* father.

"I don't think my grandfather even knew how to use a fast-food drive-through speaker," I say. "I was once with him when he tried to order at a Wendy's. He started yelling for boiled eggs in all directions. Didn't even bother to roll down the car window."

Our grandfathers could have no more predicted this world than we can predict the world of our grandchildren.

"Hush up, Grandpa," they will one day tell us. "I'm trying to watch *Vomiting with the Stars*." And then they will go back to staring up at the clouds.

Space and Mass

(37 weeks)

SUNDAY.

On my way to the CBC cafeteria for lunch, I stop into the men's room to wash my hands. The hand dryer is so weak that every time I use it, I can't help closing my eyes and pretending that an asthmatic old man is blowing on my hands.

In this flight of fancy, the man's name is Doc and he sits on a stool dispensing old-timey wisdoms while lamenting the good old days of steam blimps and ankle-to-forehead muslin underwear.

"I'm the last practitioner of a dying profession," Doc laments between huffs and puffs. "With all these modern continual-cloth towel dispensers, I'll soon be going the way of the elevator boy and the seltzer lad."

After close to a minute, I give up and wipe my hands on the ends of my shirt.

I return to my desk with Salisbury steak only to realize that I've forgotten the cutlery. I search my desk drawer for a fork and knife, but succeed in finding only a teaspoon.

Eating an entire steak dinner with a plastic teaspoon proves an interesting challenge. Halfway through the meal, I become curious about the Salisbury steak's etymology. After consulting Wikipedia, I learn it was invented by a Dr. James Henry Salisbury, an MD during the Civil War. The doctor believed that vegetables were responsible for "heart disease, tumours, mental illness, and tuberculosis" and that his steak dish, when eaten three times a day with coffee, could be healthful and also serve as a cure for battle-induced diarrhea.

Finishing the last spoonful, I hope that, at the very least, it's cured me of my desire for dessert.

Ten minutes later, back in the cafeteria, I see it has not.

MONDAY.

The local repertory house is playing *2001: A Space Odyssey*. While watching, I notice three things of interest: 1, while Hilton Hotels and Howard Johnsons are shown to survive forty years into the future, neckties don't; 2, there is precisely one joke in the entire movie. One of the characters, about to use a space toilet, is confronted by a placard containing complex Ikea-like instructions regarding its operation; and 3, the monolith looks an awful lot like an iPhone.

The person in the seat in front of me is eating McDonald's, and as a result I'm unconsciously experiencing outer space as a place that smells of Big Macs. This kind of thing has happened to me before. While watching *Das Boot*, the person beside me was wearing Polo cologne, which made the submarine smell like a sports bar.

When the movie is done, I find myself in the mood for something only slightly less sublime than outer space: a Big Mac. I will eat it with thoughts about space, the future of man, and the curative power of ground beef rattling around my head like empty soda cans on a late-night metro car.

THURSDAY.

Tucker and I are sitting on my couch, passing a container of Häagen-Dazs back and forth.

"Wouldn't it be great if the Canadian dollar and the Canadian calorie were somehow linked?" he asks.

"How do you mean?"

"Like when the American dollar is weak, American calories would also become weak. So when a hundred Canadian calories are the same as eighty-two American calories, the time would be right to go over the border, rent a motel room, and spend the weekend eating pizza and doughnuts."

"And then the moment you cross back into Canada, you instantly get fatter?" I ask.

"Yes, but since we weigh ourselves in kilograms, we can still believe ourselves fit."

Whatever happened to those 2001 moon colonies we were promised—a place where we could eat ice cream all day and still bounce around as light as lunar dust? Sometimes I just can't stand the unbearable fatness of being.

Real Tears, Finally

(36 weeks)

MONDAY, 7:00 A.M.

I've decided to spend Christmas vacation in New York City. During the course of the eleven-hour train ride, I pass the time eavesdropping. The best thing I overhear is a large man in a Miami Dolphins cap explain how, in the middle of writing a cheque for a Jacuzzi down payment, his pen ran out of ink. He saw it as a sign from God not to buy a Jacuzzi.

"When the Almighty raises a hand, I obey," he said.

1:00 P.M.

As people on the train begin to doze, I throw *It's a Wonderful Life* into my laptop, and by the end of the movie there are tears streaming down my face. Success! With my cheeks still wet, I run down the aisle to the washroom to see what I look like crying. Not bad.

I believe that the world breaks down into two groups: those who want to see what they look like crying and those who do not. For some reason, most of the people I befriend seem to fall into the former group—a group that never fully throw themselves into the moment, but always hold on to a little bit of narrative objectivity, even at their gloomiest.

7:00 P.M.

The train arrives in Penn Station, and I set off to meet Starlee, who I'll be staying with. When I get to the bistro, she is standing by the bar talking to a semi-well-known comic. Shortly after introducing us, the semi-well-known comic leaves and I take his seat. I order a scotch and water, and after several sips, notice the drink tastes rather watery. This is because it's the glass of water the semi-well-known comic has left behind. In a panic, I blot my tongue with cocktail napkins. While an entertaining bunch, comedians as a group do not impress me as adhering to the highest code of hygiene.

Starlee continues telling me a story, but I'm not able to pay much attention as I'm distracted by the thought that I may now have hepatitis—or at the very least a bad case of the cooties.

11:30 P.M.

I read the semi–well–known comic's Wikipedia entry and there is no mention of contagious diseases. I tell myself everything will be fine.

TUESDAY, 3:00 A.M.

I awake convinced that I'm in the throes of a fever sweat brought on by the onset of mononucleosis, an illness of which I have only the vaguest understanding. I turn on the lights, and look it up on Wikipedia.

9:00 A.M.

There's a knock at the door. I roll off the couch and answer it. It's Ruby, Starlee's fifteen–year–old intern.

"Why in God's name do you have an intern?" I ask when Ruby leaves the room to go sort Starlee's bookshelf.

"I have a lot to impart," she says.

Starlee is working on a self-help book called *It Is Your Fault*, and Ruby has been booking appointments all week with psychics, behaviourists, and self-professed shamans for Starlee's research. Ruby carries around a dog-eared copy of *The Bell Jar* and a notebook she uses to write down the little bits of wisdom that Starlee imparts.

Ruby re-enters the room and Starlee begins to impart.

"Choose your college based on where the cutest boys are," Starlee says, and Ruby takes furious notes.

I find myself struggling to come up with a couple wise things, in the hope of making it into the notebook.

"When buying cottage cheese," I say, "always reach to the very back of the shelf."

Ruby nods politely, the notebook closed on her lap.

We all sit around the kitchen table, surrounded by last night's beer bottles, eating pretzels for breakfast while Starlee dispenses life lessons: "Read Joan Didion. Don't let skinny girls depress you."

Eventually Starlee's wisdoms will run dry and she will have Ruby walk her dog and defrost her freezer.

When Ruby leaves the room, I reach for her notebook. Flipping it open, I write: "The line between an internship and a kidnapping can often be blurry."

SATURDAY.

I decide to fly back to Montreal, and on the plane I'm seated beside a little girl reading *Little House in the Big Woods*. This is the first book I ever read, and seeing it again, in this little girl's hands, makes me feel misty. This in spite of the fact I hated the book so much that it almost turned me off reading altogether.

There's just something about flying that always makes me a little emotional, makes me feel my own mortality in a very particular way. Perhaps it's the way everything looks so small from up here. Or perhaps it's the way that turbulence makes me feel, in the pit of my stomach, the tenuousness of life. More than likely though, it's probably due to the double bourbon I always have when I fly. There should be a word for this feeling. Call it *bourboulent*.

New Year's

(35 weeks)

WEDNESDAY, 7:10 P.M.

Tucker calls to see what I'm doing for New Year's Eve.

"Catching up on my reading," I say. "I'm going to be forty soon and I've only read one Tolstoy novel. No, New Year's is kid's stuff."

"Come on. I'll make you a sash and you can pretend to be the baby new year," he says. "It'll make you feel young."

After putting down the phone, I can't bring myself to read Tolstoy. I instead reach for the Stephen King novel I keep on the TV for when the cable goes off. I begin with the dedication page and find myself wondering if, after so many dozens of books, Stephen King fears running out of family and friends to dedicate his work to. Perhaps he'll soon have to start making dedications to casual acquaintances, like the guy who holds the door open for him at his local convenience store. When he has to start dedicating books to people he can't even stand, he may realize it's time to get out of the writing business.

8:30 P.M.

Marie-Claude phones to see if I want to come over and celebrate with her and the kids.

"Celebrate what?" I ask. "The march to the grave?"

"You know, you can afford to be a little more receptive to the world around you."

"Next time I'm in a restroom I'll keep the stall door open to shake hands and pass out business cards."

"Baby steps," she says. "Next time you're in a restroom just try washing your hands."

9:45 P.M.

My mother calls. When I tell her I'm not going out, she starts to worry.

"You're sick," she says. "You sound nasal."

"I was born nasal. I'm just not in the mood. It's not a big deal."

"Even your father's having a party," she says.

She explains that, as we speak, he's seated at the kitchen table, eating crackers and listening to the radio.

"And not talk radio, but the music kind," she says. "Let him have his fun. It's New Year's, after all."

10:30 P.M.

Tony phones from his future in-laws.

"I'm not doing anything," I say, pre-emptively. "It's going to be a new year tomorrow whether Jonathan Goldstein dances on a coffee table with a lampshade on his head or not."

"You remind me of a girl I once dated who always fast-forwarded through the opening credits when we watched videos," he says.

"She sounds like a keeper."

"We broke up after two weeks," he says. "It could have probably lasted at least a month or two, but she fast-forwarded us. The point is, you can't rush to the end. Life shouldn't be about that."

We get off the phone. I hit the metaphorical pause button and stare out the window.

11:15 P.M.

Characters in books and on TV shows often learn about what really matters in life through the guidance of helpful supernatural beings who know more than we mortals ever will. Take Scrooge in *A Christmas Carol*, for instance, or the family from *Alf*.

Staring out the window, I consider how in real life, all we've got are our hunches about what matters. And, of course, we also have our family and friends to steer us a little when we've a hunch our hunches are wrong.

Marie-Claude's probably already put the kids to bed, so I call up Tucker to see if I can still come by, and he says sure.

"I'll bring some chips," I say. "It's New Year's, after all."

Judgment
(34 weeks)

WEDNESDAY.

I'm walking over to Howard's with my newly adopted toy poodle, Boosh. My father had to give her up after my mother developed an allergy—though less a reaction to dogs, it would seem, than to the loss of my father's attention. Boosh, she claimed, reminded her of another drain on my father's attention: Judge Judy.

"How can a dog remind you of Judge Judy?" I asked.

"She gives me a judgy look," my mother said.

At a red light, one of those outlaw motorcycles pulls up alongside us. The rider revs his engine and I feel my testes inch their way into my throat. I'm sure the sound stirs something primordial, something akin to what our caveman ancestors must have felt while being chased by mastodons.

I flash the motorcyclist one of the most withering looks in my arsenal, the one I deploy only in extreme situations, like when confronting teenagers jumping the line. That he does not get off his hog and imprint the "Life Is a Gamble" belt buckle into the back of my calves attests to the power of walking around with a toy poodle. A toy poodle is like wearing spectacles in the 1940s, or being rolled through the city in an iron lung: it is a declaration of your power-lessness. Which can be powerful.

I arrive at Howard's.

"What's that thing around Boosh's neck?" he asks.

"A cape," I say.

"Are you going to teach her how to bark in a Romanian accent?" he asks.

Howard is being sarcastic, though not as hurtfully so as Gregor, who yesterday suggested I get rid of the cape because it was making my poodle's ass look fat.

Howard pulls out his grocery bag of takeout menus. He decides on what we'll be having for lunch by sloshing his arm around in it and withdrawing a lucky winner.

"Looks like it's chops," he says. "Lamb or pork?"

In my old high school, girls who were turning sixteen had a choice between two gifts for their "sweet": a nose job or a trip to Europe. I find myself sympathetic to what those poor girls had to go through. There are certain things no person should ever have to choose between, and so I urge Howard to order both.

FRIDAY.

I'm out for dinner with my family. My father proposed the meal so that he could be updated on Boosh's doings. I fill him in on all the whitefish she's been eating and garbage she's been destroying, and when that's out of the way, we move on to my father's second favourite topic of conversation.

"Did you watch *Judge Judy* today?" he asks. "Boy, a mouth on her!"

"Here we go," my mother says. "Judge Judy is his girlfriend."

"She is not," my father says, reddening.

"He's always had a crush on Judy," my sister says. She is pregnant and her amusement makes her seem Buddha-like.

"I hope you know she's had a lot of work done," my mother says. "If you think that's her real face, you're sadly mistaken."

"The name of this restaurant sounds familiar," I say, turning to my mother. "Is this the place where they called the police on you?"

"That was over a month ago," she says, waving her hand dismissively. "And they didn't call the police. They *threatened* to call the police. I refuse to pay for salmon steak when having distinctly ordered salmon fillet."

"And you don't feel uncomfortable coming back?"

"They gave me a ten-dollar coupon for the confusion. How else can I use it?"

In his sixteenth-century epic *Monkey*, Wu Ch'êng-ên writes, "He who fails to avenge the wrongs done to a parent is unworthy of the name of man."

When my salmon fillet arrives I eat it, not feeling like a man so much as a giant salmon-eating porpoise. But then suddenly, the spirit of avenging justice descends. It is empowering and emphatic.

"If my father says he doesn't have the hots for Judge Judy," I say, "then that's it. End of story."

I finish the remaining bites of my meal, a man once more.

A Mission

(33 weeks)

I open the front door and my mother hands me four cases of yogurt. All strawberry. She doesn't notice flavours. Coffee, vanilla, blueberry—they don't mean a thing. I ask her how much I owe her, and she tells me that with the coupons, and how she used them on double-down day, she actually made money off the purchase. I tell her I don't see how such a thing is possible, and she explains that the yogurts were a buck apiece and her coupons were for seventy-five cents. Doubled, that's a dollar fifty.

"I make fifty cents off each one I buy," she says.

She's excited because she has a project for the two of us: a defective shirt that needs exchanging. She got it from a clothing store near my house that's been around for decades. When I was a kid, my mother would take me there to buy shoes, making me take my pants off first for some reason, right in the aisle, before trying them on.

"What's wrong with the shirt?" I ask.

"It's missing a sleeve," she says. "How can I let your father leave the house like that? No way."

It should be said that my father has left the house in worse: green corduroy vests, T-shirts advertising aquarium supplies, ties intended for novelty use only. If it were handed to him as he was getting out of a shower, I'm sure my father would figure out a way to wear a bridge chair.

I ask how a missing sleeve might have escaped her notice during the purchase. She doesn't remember. She bought it a long time ago.

"How long ago?" I ask.

She doesn't really get the question. Life for my mother isn't exactly a chronological unravelling. She was coming to visit me. I'm around the corner from the store. It's just a clever thing to return it now—killing two birds with one stone. She looks at the bag and thinks for a moment.

"Five years," she says.

This kind of operation is what my mother lives for. It would be a challenge, a battle of wills—a game of chess, but with yelling. I remember as a kid watching her open three bottles of tahini, one after the other. She wasn't satisfied with the hermetic popping sound the caps made—it was too muted. She liked a pop that was more emphatic, a pop that cried, "I have not been sprinkled with hemlock." She returned all of them to a grocery store she'd chosen, not because she bought the tahini there, but because of its proximity to our house. The store didn't sell tahini. I'm not sure they even knew what it was.

To be honest, it isn't that my mother exerts Clarence Darrow–like powers of persuasion; it's that she has no shame. None at all. As an adult, I seem to have taken on the extra shame she has no use for. I don't like to draw attention to myself. If a waitress gets my order wrong, I keep my mouth shut. If a bus driver goes past my stop, I just get off at the next one. Scenes just aren't my thing. But even now, no matter where I go with my mother, there are always the inevitable spectacles. Just the thought of her getting all froth-mouthed about that one-armed shirt—it was enough to make me queasy.

10:40 A.M.

At the store, my mother heads to the cash register and pulls the article of clothing out of the crumpled plastic bag.

"It's missing a sleeve," she says to the saleswoman.

The saleswoman looks at it. Holds it up. Turns it around.

"It doesn't have sleeves," the saleswoman says. "It's a poncho."

"A pon-cho?" my mother repeats, as though it's a foreign word—which, in her defence, I guess it sort of is.

You'd think that would be the end of it, that my mother would accept the fact that we live in a universe where such a thing as a poncho exists, and we would leave.

But this is not to happen. Reason is of no concern in a staring contest.

"I don't care what it is," she says evenly. "It's factory-defective. My husband can't wear it."

I thought of my father, a man very big on tucking in clothes—sweaters, aquarium-supply T-shirts—packing the bottom of the poncho into his pants, belting up, and heading out for an evening on the town looking like Fatty Arbuckle.

The saleswoman refuses to give the money back, so my mother asks her to get the manager and the woman disappears behind a row of suit jackets.

10:50 A.M.

As we wait, I remain by my mother's side, standing there in this way I developed as a kid. It's a posture that's meant to convey filial loyalty peppered with a touch of what Vietnam vets call the thousand-yard stare.

In the back room, I imagine the saleswoman conferring with the manager, a bedraggled, shiny-jowled man, as he stares at my mother through a security cam, watching with a look of recognition that quickly turns to panic.

10:55 A.M.

The saleswoman returns, immediately offering store credit.

That's a mistake. Weakness.

"Credit? So you can unload socks on us?" my mother asks. "We need more socks like we need rickets."

Desperate to defuse the situation, I grab a baseball cap off a nearby shelf and hand it to my mother. Reluctantly, she gets it for me with her credit.

"Lucky for you my boy needs a hat," she says. "Walk around in it. Make sure it isn't too tight around the temples."

As we leave the store together, my new cap on my head, I feel about ten years old.

"I'll hold on to the receipt," my mother says. "Just in case."

A Thousand Monkeys and Darwin

(32 weeks)

MONDAY.

I'm sick in bed. I wish I had some apple juice and Spider-Man comics, but for now I'd settle for Kleenex. I call up Howard to bring some over.

"Use toilet paper," he says.

"That'd be unseemly for a man of my social carriage," I say.

"Hey, did I tell you about my idea for a new twist on toilet paper?" Howard asks, sounding as though he's leaning into the receiver. "It's toilet paper that has the face of someone you hate printed on each square."

Howard goes on to explain how his invention could mean the end of school bullying, gangland violence, and possibly, even war.

"Just ball up your detractors and wipe," he says. "I

believe I've always done my finest work behind the backs of my enemies. Now they can do their finest work behind mine."

We get off the phone and I get some toilet paper to blow my nose. With no enemies defaced, it almost feels like a waste of my effort.

TUESDAY.

My cold has not gotten better, so I lie in bed and watch Jerry Lewis's *The Ladies Man*. In one scene, Lewis's character, Herbert H. Heebert, is being force-fed baby food while strapped into a high chair. The scene has the look of something that's been directed by a thousand monkeys seated behind a thousand movie cameras. While the movie proves not to be very good, it is, in parts, stunningly beautiful to watch—the sets, the colours—and there are moments of almost perfect absurdity.

Beginning to feel guilty about not getting enough rest, I stop the film, but just before I do, Lewis, in an uncharacteristic moment of lucidity, says wistfully, "Being alone can be very lonely. At least with people around, you can be lonely with noise."

Wisdom can come from the most unexpected places, and no place is more unexpected than the spastic, baby food–encrusted mouth of Jerry Lewis.

WEDNESDAY.

Lonely, still sick, and without anything to make lunch with, I call up Tony to see if he'll bring me over some food.

"All I've got is half a bag of Fritos and some pickles," I say.

"You should forget about lunch and just snack," he says. "Snacking is a very evolved human endeavour."

"How's that?"

"I just saw a news report about how in three billion years, a day will be a month long. So with breakfast being two weeks away from dinner, and dinner being two weeks away from lunch, snacking between meals will be an evolutionary necessity."

"Can you bring me over some chicken soup?" I plead.

"No dice," he says. "*Wheel of Fortune* is about to come on and I've got a bowl of cereal on my lap."

I get off the phone and open the bag of Fritos. I only wish Darwin was alive to see this.

Beginnings, Middles, and Ends
(31 weeks)

MONDAY.

Fully recovered, I've started writing a story for my radio show. It's about a man who spends the morning eating himself sick with pie only to remember—in a flash of sinus-clearing terror—that he's due to participate in a county fair pie-eating contest in an hour. He'd drunkenly challenged his ex-wife's new husband to an eat-off several weeks earlier, and now, ready to burst at the seams, he sets off to the fair to do his best.

I want it to be a parable about remaining stoic in the face of nausea. While I know it will end with his being rushed to the ER to have his stomach pumped, I'm not sure what happens in the middle.

I look over my notes. They are not helpful. One note reads "Make pie more existential."

Writer's block descends like a ... something or other.

TUESDAY.

Still unable to write the story, I take a break and read the latest *New Yorker* for inspiration. I arrive at a poem that contains the following lines:

> Seasons repeat themselves, but the tree
> Shading the yard keeps growing.

Ideally, how should a *New Yorker* poem be read? The same as you would a *New Yorker* cartoon? Because it feels inappropriate to partake in a beautiful bit of verse filled with simple, profound truths about the human condition and then return to a profile of Lady Gaga on the same page.

And so after finishing the poem, I take a walk in the snow.

WEDNESDAY.

Writer's block persists.

I decide to nap, and while asleep I dream I'm riding an old-fashioned bicycle while sporting a handlebar moustache drenched in mustard. It strikes me as a portentous omen. I awake and immediately call up Tucker to go for hot dogs.

Tucker says that hot dogs seem like a good idea, that they may buoy his spirits. He says he's been filled with so much self-loathing lately that he considers starting each day by spitting into his own coffee.

Tucker's self-revulsion might be part of a growing cultural trend—one that can inspire whole new markets of enterprise. I can imagine seeing these special coffees sold at Starbucks for five dollars a pop. Call them "prison cappuccinos."

I tell Tucker my idea and he says that if it were to bear his imprimatur, he would not want it offered with soy.

"I'm tired of hearing everyone talk about how they're switching from milk to soy. Why doesn't anyone talk about switching from milk to whisky?"

Soon Tucker will bring his trademark iconoclasm to the hot dog joint where, as usual, he will eat his wiener by alternating his bites from one end to the other end until he is left with his final, middle bite.

Tucker's hot dog technique recalls what Jean-Luc Godard had to say about film: there should always be a beginning, middle, and end—just not necessarily in that order. And like Godard, Tucker upsets expectations. So much so that the counterman, as always, watches him eat while waiting anxiously for the whole confusing spectacle to end. I watch, too, making my peace with the fact that sometimes the middle is the last thing you reach, in hot dogs as well as stories about pie-eating.

Padding the Dream
(30 weeks)

SUNDAY.

As my wallet is beginning to smell like a junkyard Barcalounger and look as misshapen as my father's, I've purchased a new one. I go through the old one and empty it of the shards of plans left undone. Business cards for services meant to improve my life, unfilled medical prescriptions meant to improve my health, and fortune-cookie fortunes that were meant to inspire me but instead only made me hungry for Chinese food. A dream deflated does not look like a raisin in the sun. It looks like an old emptied wallet.

I slide the new streamlined billfold into my back pocket, turn around to look at it there, and realize that, without a wallet full of hope, my once shapely buttocks are a thing of the past.

WEDNESDAY.

Howard and I have ordered pizza. When the delivery guy hands over the bill, Howard suggests I break in my new wallet.

The food arrives cold, so I go into the kitchen to reheat it. To my horror, I discover that my oven, which I've not opened in months, looks like the inside of a hot dog factory chimney.

THURSDAY.

My neighbour Mike calls up. He wants me to come over and eat his wife's chicken soup while Boosh pees on his living room carpet. Why? Because he's superstitious and wants to recreate the exact circumstances of my visit last month when the Montreal Canadiens beat the Florida Panthers. I tell him I can't make it, that I have an oven to clean.

FRIDAY.

I wake up and find that a small card has been tossed through my mail slot. It's from Mike.

"Thanks for making the Canadiens lose," the card reads.

I place the card in my wallet, and then tuck the wallet

into my back pocket. I walk over to the wall mirror and spin around to examine myself.

"In good time," I think, "you will have the rump of a Greek god."

Baby Steps
(29 weeks)

MONDAY.

My sister was in her late thirties when she announced her pregnancy.

"It's a miracle," my mother said. Dina Goldstein is a woman who had me in her teens, and she believes in early starts. Rising at 5:00 a.m. to dust ceiling fans and fireplace logs, she is sprung from the mould of shtetl women past who cleaned, loved, and worried with great ferocity. Which is to say, she'd been waiting to be a grandmother since her twenties. And which is also to say, with my sister's good news, the pressure was off me.

Today is the blessed day of the baby's arrival, and we all meet up at the hospital. I've never been in a room where so many members of my family are so happy all at once. Usually, maybe one or two are happy at any given time while the rest hold down the fort, remaining dyspeptic, dysphoric, or boldly struggling to maintain a nice, even level of dispiritedness.

Tolstoy once wrote that every unhappy family is unhappy in its own way and that happy families are all alike. This is not so, as evidenced by my father, who is smilingly biting into a home-brought chicken sandwich while seated atop an upturned wastepaper basket, and my mother, who is rubbing disinfectant gel onto her lips, preparing to kiss the newborn.

We all stand around for hours, happily staring at the baby and clutching our chests. How strange to feel yourself falling in love with someone you've only just met. And how endlessly fascinating it is to watch someone getting used to being alive. Though perhaps even more fascinating is watching someone get used to being a part of our family.

The male-pattern balding that starts at twelve. The foot fungus that rises up to the thighs and the hemorrhoids that descend to the ankles. Not to mention the messy eating. Legend has it that one time my father kept an egg noodle hanging from his lower lip for the duration of the Canada Day weekend. If he could only have lasted a few more days he might have ended up on the Johnny Carson show, seated on the couch alongside the guy who hiccupped for forty years.

But to look at my nephew, so little and brand new, and to even think these things feels wrong somehow. So I shoo them away and try to think only positive thoughts.

"May he enjoy nothing but happiness," I intone. Not wanting to draw attention, I intone to myself. "Days without embarrassment. Days without pain." Or, at least seven days without pain, at which time he will have the flesh at the end of his penis shorn off. After which, Dixie cups of schnapps and honey cake will be served.

THURSDAY.

Josh and I go for an after-work drink at our neighbourhood bar. Josh thinks we're getting too old for the place, that we should find a good divorcée bar to hang out at. We listen in on what the young people are talking about at the table beside us.

"My Grampy Joe," the girl says, "he bakes a potato, scoops out the insides, mixes it with cheese and then puts it back into the potato skin!"

"Sadly," says Josh, leaning into me, "'Grampy Joe' is probably a year younger than you."

FRIDAY.

At a loss for where to have dinner together, my father, newly minted "Grampy Goldstein," suggests we drive out to Ikea to dine on Swedish meatballs.

"I can use a towel holder anyway," he says.

"A towel holder?" I ask. "That's what the good Lord created doorknobs for."

At Ikea, before beginning to shop, my father stops in at the washroom. I wait for him for almost ten minutes.

"What took you so long?" I ask.

"I was waiting for someone to come in and let me out," he says. "I don't like to touch the doorknob once I've washed my hands. And now that I'm a grandfather, I have to be extra careful."

"So you just stood there, waiting?"

"Not just waiting. I worked on the Word Jumble I keep in my pocket."

As my father shops, I study the expressions on men's faces as they're led by their girlfriends and wives through Ikea. They are expressions that fall somewhere between sorrow and despair. But there's something stoic there, too, as if there's an internalized understanding that the pain of doing something you don't want to do is the essence of love. Like waiting in a bathroom doing word puzzles to protect your grandson. Or shopping for towel holders with your father.

A Covenant

(28 weeks)

MONDAY.

It's the day of my nephew's bris. It's only 5:30 a.m., but I'm very anxious about the whole thing and can't sleep. After the last bris I attended, it was days before I could pry my hands out of my front pockets. I decide to just get out of bed and make my way over to the synagogue.

I'm the first guest to arrive and so I hang out with the mohel. As he prepares his tools we make small talk, and at a certain point he tells me why he got into "moheling," but before he can get very far, and with my heart racing because I know it might be the only time I'll ever get the chance to use this line on an actual mohel, I blurt out, "For the tips?"

The mohel doesn't laugh, which doesn't make sense to me. The context is perfect and my timing, impeccable. I conclude that to be a good mohel, you must always be on guard against the peril of shaking with laughter.

When things begin, I sit as far away from the proceedings as I can. By contrast, all the pre-adolescent girls have taken up the entire front row. They're too young to gain admittance into horror films, so this must be the next best thing. Their faces are a mix of anticipation and delight. One of them looks as though she might start moshing.

Someone should make a coffee table book composed of photos of little girls watching brises. It could be called *Thank God I'm a Girl*.

TUESDAY.

I receive an email invitation to lunch from my neighbour Mike, the Canadiens fan. The subject heading reads "Lunch Baby Lunch." There is no punctuation, but I find myself reading it as "Lunch: Baby Lunch." What this brings to mind is a high-end, high-concept restaurant called "Baby Lunch," a place where the diner would be seated in a high chair, fitted into a bonnet and bib, and then spoon-fed beef tartare by a tuxedoed waiter.

"Here comes the monsieur's choo-choo."

Mike's office is near mine, so we meet at a new restaurant in the area. The meal is good and so is the service, but with "Café Baby Lunch" still on my mind, I can't help feeling a little disappointed that the wait staff only goes so far as placing the food on the table and not in your mouth.

"Ever wonder what it would feel like to be burped after a meal?" I ask Mike, and judging by his silence, it would seem he has not. Still, the image of two full grown men burping each other in a restaurant parking lot is, to me, a funny one. I think an easy formula for comedy is this: men treated like babies equals comedy. Except in the case of circumcision. And Jerry Lewis.

Two for One
(27 weeks)

MONDAY.

A few days after Valentine's Day, while waiting for the bus, I discover a folded piece of Hilroy notebook paper in a snowbank. I open it and at the top of the paper, written in green pen, is the title "The Reasons Why I Did Not Kiss Her Back." The reasons are listed in descending order of importance:

5. Because I was so drunk that looking at her up close was making me dizzy.
4. Because I wanted her to see that even though she thinks she's all that, she isn't all that.
3. Because I was really into the movie and didn't want to miss any of it.
2. Because I'm dating her cousin.
1. Because her lips were greasy from chicken nuggets.

TUESDAY.

While eating chicken nuggets at my desk, I wonder whether fast food restaurants still give out paper party hats and whether they would give one to an adult. I'm not sure whether eating chicken nuggets at my desk while wearing a cardboard crown would make me feel less sad or more sad, but I am sure I would eat with my office door shut.

THURSDAY.

Marie-Claude and I are out for an early breakfast. Eating grape jelly makes us nostalgic for childhood.

"When I was a kid," I say, "I thought I'd grow up and eat bacon every day. I couldn't understand why any sane person wouldn't."

"When I was a kid, I wanted to be successful," Marie-Claude says, "and I thought successful people ate only caviar and champagne. That's the eighties for you."

"When I was a kid, I thought the only way a man could let a woman know he liked her was by winking at her. Because I couldn't wink, I thought I'd be alone for the rest of my life. I'd sit in my room for hours, trying so hard to wink I'd almost throw up."

"Now there's a way to attract a mate," Marie-Claude says. "Vomiting. It's just like a peacock spreading its tail."

"I've heard some birds mate for life," I say. "Like pigeons. I guess it makes me like them more than I would otherwise."

"Did you know that in Sweden it's illegal to sell a guinea pig that isn't in a pair?"

"It'd be nice if humans came that way, too."

FRIDAY.

I'm watching a member of the Maasai tribe in Kenya on the news. He is a warrior who operates a program called the Lion Guardians. The intention of the project is to protect cattle while not killing lions, which are now endangered in Africa.

The reporter asks the man why he started the program.

"To impress women," he answers.

Building the Parthenon? Crossing the Delaware? Forget about it. If it wasn't for impressing women, nothing would ever get done.

I wonder if a male peacock ever woke up one morning and realized just how obvious he was being, the way a man can. To realize too much makes the world less colourful.

SATURDAY.

I'm out doing errands while wearing my Cossack's hat. What with the burning down of the villages and whatnot, we do not much admire the Cossacks, but we do admire their hats. I find that wearing a Cossack's hat brings a certain regality to the performance of mundane tasks—things like doing errands, or cleaning up after a poodle.

For years I could never wear mine because it was too tight for my head, but since having shaved my hair, it fits perfectly. Also nice is that it makes me feel like I still have hair. It's kind of like "The Gift of the Magi" without all the cruel irony.

When I get home, I throw the hat onto the couch and put away the groceries, and when I return to the living room, I find Boosh curled up with it, looking, for all intents and purposes, like she's finally found a soulmate.

SOULMATES

Before he ever moved to Gotham City, before he grew into the overweight, obsessive sad sack of his later years, The Penguin was a poet and a dandy who lived in London. He wrote complex villanelles and threw lavish dinner parties at which he only became more charming the more he drank. He wore a monocle, a top hat, and carried an umbrella.

One evening at one of his dinner parties, after hours spent sipping absinthe, The Penguin ran up to the roof of his building, opened up his large black umbrella, and leapt off into the air. As he coasted to the ground, he hollered out lines from Blake, stuff about grabbing life by the fat of its stomach and giving it a twist. He was that crazy. He was that bursting with life.

From that night on he made it his habit to jump off roofs, ever higher, while clutching an umbrella.

After a while he got pretty good at it, too. He saw that by kicking his legs and twisting his back a certain way, he could actually prolong his flight, coasting all over the place, sometimes landing only after several daring minutes aloft.

It came to pass that The Penguin started hearing more and more about a certain nanny named Mary Poppins. She, too, he was told, had been floating around London hanging from an umbrella handle. Everywhere he went The Penguin kept hearing about her, how it was simply insane that they had not yet met each other.

So finally a dinner party was arranged by someone who knew them both, and on the evening of the party, The Penguin walked into the drawing room, saw Mary Poppins on the divan, doffed his top hat, and bowed low, as was his style in those days.

He had planned a few things to say and do when first meeting Mary Poppins. He thought he might lift up his umbrella as though challenging her to a duel. He imagined she would smile and take up her own frilly, perhaps pink umbrella and then, together, they would dance about the room, leaping over furniture, parrying and thrusting, perhaps even winding things up breathing heavily, nose to nose.

Instead what happened was The Penguin became very shy and quiet. As he stood there staring at her, his top hat felt needlessly clumsy and his monocle too small for his face; plus, the squinting needed to keep it in place was giving him a slight headache. For the first time in his life, The Penguin felt ludicrous.

"I imagine you two must have an infinite amount of things to speak of," said their host as he sat them together at the dinner table. The Penguin nodded nervously.

After three or four minutes it became clear that The Penguin and Mary Poppins had absolutely nothing to say to each other that did not deal exclusively with umbrella travel—getting stuck in trees, the shoulder aches, the anxiety about tipping over in the wind.

Everyone at the table just sat there staring at them expectantly, which made the whole thing even more awkward.

Trying to move things along, Mary Poppins asked The Penguin if he liked to sing, to which The Penguin responded, "Only when I'm drunk." Then she asked if he enjoyed children, to which he replied, "Yes, in a sweet wine sauce."

The Penguin then asked Mary Poppins how she kept people from looking up her skirt when she flew. She smiled politely, then turned to the man on her left and asked him how he was enjoying the lamb.

The man on her left was wearing an elegant, aristocratic cape. Mary, a bit drunk on the sherry, noted that if he spread his cape out he might be able to glide about like a bat. The man on her left chuckled and suggested that after dinner they head up to the roof and give it a try, which they did.

Honeymoon for One
(26 weeks)

SATURDAY.

"So you're off to Puerto Rico," my friends say.

"You mean Poo-errrto Rrrico," I say, rolling my tongue with sensual languor. This is one of the many reasons why I do not have a lot of friends; but it's true: I'm off to San Juan for a week-long holiday.

Lately I've been spending so much time sitting at my desk that I fear I've become some kind of Greek mythological beast—half man, half office chair.

I polled my friends and family for a suitable destination, but in the end, it was my parents who won me over. Puerto Rico it was—the place where they spent their honeymoon in 1966.

Before leaving, I call them up to pick their brains for some indication of things I should see and do. My mother answers, and I tell her to have my father pick up the extension. He's in the middle of watching *Jeopardy*, but he does so, begrudgingly.

"What did you know about Puerto Rico before you went there?" I ask.

"That it's where Puerto Ricans come from," my mother says uncertainly.

"There's a soda shop on San Felipe Street that makes an egg cream to drop dead for," my father says. "Ask for Little Pepe."

"That was over forty years ago," my mother yells. "Little Pepe's probably a skeleton hanging in a Puerto Rican high school biology class."

Before getting off the phone, I tell them that a part of this trip is a tribute to them. And their love. A love that bore me.

"That's nice," my mother says.

"Who is Henry Kissinger?" my father says.

SUNDAY.

My flight leaves at 6:00 a.m. and, in keeping with the alacrity and caution of my ancestry, I've arrived at the airport three and a half hours early. As a result, I'm functioning on about fifteen minutes' sleep.

Onboard the flight it's too early for whisky. So I order a Heineken, which helps steady my sleep-deprived nerves for flying. It's always been my belief that if we were meant to fly, we'd have been born with fold-out food trays embedded in our backs.

In San Juan, I unpack my bags in the same hotel that my parents stayed in and head down to the hotel casino, where I decide to join a game of bingo—or what the hotel calls Bingie, Bingie. ("Sounds fancier," the woman calling the numbers explains.)

My adversaries are three women in their seventies, and after twenty-five minutes of fierce combat, my heart racing, I cry out, "Bingie, Bingie!" I am so exhilarated that my voice almost cracks.

The only thing sadder than a grown man on a honeymoon with himself triumphantly calling out "Bingie, Bingie" is that same man *mistakenly* calling out "Bingie, Bingie." It seems I mistook an *ocho* for a *nueve*.

"No Bingie, Bingie?" I ask, no longer exhilarated, and my competitors nod and smile at me with good-natured, holiday-spirited *schadenfreude*.

MONDAY.

I've spent the whole day eating so much Puerto Rican food that I dare not enter the hotel pool for fear of cramping. So when I haven't been eating—which really couldn't have been for more than fifteen minutes of my waking day—I spend my time in the hot tub, a body of water probably invented for people too full to swim. I consider getting myself one of those arm floaties and wearing it like a neck brace, so I can doze in the tub without drowning after a large meal of tamales.

TUESDAY.

I'm told there's always something going on at night in the hotel lobby, and there is. In the middle of the ballroom-size room, I find a woman in her mid-sixties dancing with a man in plaid shorts and suspenders.

I can't help wondering what my parents might have looked like dancing here all those years ago. I've only seen them dance at bar mitzvahs, where my father does this kind of kung fu kicking thing and my mother frantically hops from foot to foot as though standing outside an occupied toilet stall.

I find a pay phone in the lobby and call Montreal.

"What's the matter?" my mother asks.

"Nothing's the matter," I say. "I was just wondering whether you and Dad danced when you were in San Juan."

"Your father made me," she says. "He and his brother Sheldon took classes at the Arthur Murray dance school. One of the seminars was on the cha-cha."

"I never knew Dad took dance lessons," I say.

"Your father was always afraid of being a wallflower," she says.

Before we get off the phone she asks me what number sunblock I'm using.

"Seventy," I say.

"Don't be a hero," she says. "Get ninety."

As the music blares, I imagine taking off my jacket and whirling it above my head like a helicopter propeller. I imagine doing one of those life-affirming, leg-kicking things. But in the end, I find a nice wall against which I allow my inner wallflower to blossom.

WEDNESDAY.

I've booked a trip to the Río Grande to see the rainforest.

Our tour guide is a man named Hector. Hector starts many of his proclamations with "In Puerto Rico, we have a saying," as in, "In Puerto Rico, we have a saying: A grape is a raisin that forgot to die."

Almost none of these sayings make any sense. But still, Hector makes learning fun. As we ride through the countryside, he teaches our small group a little Puerto Rican history.

"We imported snakes to Puerto Rico to eat our rats," he says from the front of the truck, "but the snakes got out of control, so we imported mongooses to eat the snakes. But they all come out at different times in the day, so now we have rats, snakes, *and* mongooses."

Back at the hotel, I email a picture of myself beside a rainforest waterfall to Gregor.

Five minutes later, the phone in my hotel room rings.

"Why're you wearing white leotards under your shorts?" Gregor asks when I pick up the phone.

"How'd you get this number?"

"And why are you wearing a man purse?"

"It's a travel bag," I say. "I keep all my important documents in there."

As Gregor goes on, I open my laptop so that I can study the photo along with him. In it, I stand before one of the most beautiful natural waterfalls I've ever experienced, yet all I can see is my inability to properly accessorize.

THURSDAY.

With my vacation nearing an end, I sit at the hotel bar watching the Lakers play on TV.

A couple in their early twenties is seated beside me. The woman chastises the man for eating bar peanuts.

"They're nasty," she says.

As we get to talking, they share with me the details of their relationship. They had a fling and she ended up pregnant, then they split up; but after their son's first birthday, they started dating again. This is their very first trip together.

I tell them about how my parents had their honeymoon here, and as I do, it occurs to me that they're sort of on a honeymoon, too. I tell them this and they both smile.

"I guess we are," he says, reaching for a peanut.

"How romantic," she says, taking it out of his hand.

I try to imagine my parents here, kids in 1966, still doing what they always do—bickering, watching TV in bed—except wearing tropical cabana wear and travel money belts cinched so tight they can hardly breathe.

FRIDAY.

Back home in Montreal, I call up my parents.

"Do you still feel like the same people you originally fell in love with?" I ask.

They both say no.

"Your father was so good-looking then," my mother says.

"What becomes of a person," my father says.

"Don't say that," my mother says. "You're still good-looking. Better looking. Back then I liked the cologne he wore and the way he looked. But now I really love him. Now I know what kind of a person he is."

"How long did it take to find out?" I ask.

"A long time," she says. "But it grows every day. He's become like my mother and father."

She asks if I understand and I tell her I'm not sure.

"I've known him longer than I knew them," she says. "He looks out for me. Now I'm going to cry."

"What is the Suez Canal?" my father asks.

"Still with that show! 'What's this and what's that'!"

"It's almost over."

"It's always almost over!"

I put down the phone and start unpacking.

The Power of the Written Word

(25 weeks)

SUNDAY.

I've gained five pounds in Puerto Rico, and so I join the YMCA near my house.

My favourite station in the workout is the water fountain. About to take a drink, I read the sign above it.

"Don't spit in the fountain."

One of the problems with seeing someone spit in a fountain is that it makes you think about spit when you just want to be drinking water. The same can be said of a sign that reads "Don't spit in the fountain."

As I drink, I try to fill my mind with random things to blot out thoughts of spit. A suitcase full of bird whistles. A pony soaked in ketchup.

Sometimes knowing how to read can be a burden.

THURSDAY.

A physical burden, too. In a last-minute bid for erudition before middle age, I've begun reading *War and Peace*, and schlepping it along to read on my metro ride to work feels like a part of my new workout regimen.

As I'm only on page three, I fear my fellow commuters are silently judging me, thinking I look neither smart enough nor committed enough to make it all the way through. Being on page three feels like a public failure.

There's something inherently embarrassing about starting things—new jobs, gym memberships, new books. There should be a press that publishes books with a couple dozen blank pages at the beginning so it never has to look like you've just begun.

FRIDAY.

At the café table where I'm seated, someone has knifed the word "beer" into the tabletop. The letters are small and look like the product of a focused, if not slightly deranged, mind. It's a hard wood and must have taken time, determination, and great daring. The engraver was not content to stop halfway at "be," not one to convince himself, penknife-hand sore, that the word had a certain existential elegance. No, he persevered, risking a possible police record. And for what? So that I may look upon his handiwork and think: beer.

Sometimes being able to read is a good thing, and at home, I ensure that the engraver's written campaign is heeded well into the evening.

SATURDAY.

I'm at my parents' house with a hangover. I'm helping them clear space. As such, I spend the day holding up objects, asking if I can throw them out, and being told, no.

A decades-old almanac? It's bloated with water damage, as if it was last read in the shower.

My father shakes his head.

"It's a keepsake from the year your sister was born," he says. "I can't throw that out." He drops it into the "save" pile.

We rummage through laundry baskets and shoeboxes loaded with VCR instruction manuals, expired toaster warranties, and pens empty of ink since the nineties.

"Look what I found," my father says, a jewellery box in his hand.

He passes it over and I open it. There's a key chain inside that says "Christian Dyor."

"It's a Christian Dior," he says.

"It's a key chain," I say, "plus it's a fake."

Still, it makes it into the save pile.

By evening, we still haven't begun cleaning up anything. Sure the day's been a failure, but at least it's been a private one.

Irreversible

(24 weeks)

SUNDAY.

Tucker lives around the corner from me, but he doesn't like to leave the house very often, so I introduce him to video chatting. After getting him to install the appropriate software, within minutes I'm staring into my computer screen and Tucker is staring back. The experience is unexpectedly unsettling, but I still try to convince Tucker of its virtues.

"See?" I ask. "If chatting on the phone is like a game of chess, then video chatting is like a game of three-dimensional chess."

"I've always thought chatting with you in any form as being more like a game of Sorry!," he says. "Can we stop this?"

"I guess so," I say. "I'm not too crazy about your 'listening face' anyway."

"What you're seeing is my 'pretending-to-listen face,'" he says, "and either you've got poppy seeds in your teeth or I really have to clean my computer screen."

Sometimes when you stare into the abyss, the abyss stares back; at other times, it is Tucker who stares back. I'm not sure which fills me with more angst.

WEDNESDAY.

I meet Gregor for soup. I show up in my new vest which, I'm informed, makes me look like a children's entertainer.

"Strike that," he says. "A children's entertainer's monkey."

"It's reversible," I say meekly, not exactly sure why I'm defending myself. "And vests are practical, what with all the pockets."

"So when you strip down to eat a mango, the vest stays on or off? With it on, you have a place to keep your tooth-picks and paring knife."

"What are you talking about?"

"Didn't you once tell me you hate making a mess with mangos, so you eat them naked in your bathtub?"

"No. No I didn't."

"And what is this? Your five hundredth vest? Keep going this way and you'll end up on that TV show about hoarders."

"What are you talking about? This is the first vest I've ever owned in my life."

"If you can manage to get a little more famous, I can pitch the network on a *Hoarders* celebrity edition. The first episode could be Bret Michaels swimming waist-deep in bandanas, cross-cut with you trying to decide which of your twenty thousand vests to wear while eating a mango in your bathtub."

FRIDAY.

Tony and I meet for coffee downtown. He's carrying a bag from Victoria's Secret, a present for his fiancée.

"When you work in a lingerie store," he says, "you're inevitably seen as being beautiful enough to work in a lingerie store, or not beautiful enough. You're always going to be judged against the dainties."

"There's something about your saying 'dainties' that doesn't sit right."

"I'd make a good lingerie store worker," Tony says dreamily. "Sitting on a stool, telling it like it is between bites of my sandwich. 'That thong really brings out the blue in your eyes.'"

"The fashion world can really use a man like you," I say.

"Of which," Tony says, looking me over with distaste, "what's up with the vest? You look like Emo Philips."

As Tony rips into me, I settle back into my chair and brace myself. Unlike your finer quality vests, the subtle dynamics of old friendships are not reversible.

It Can't Be That Bad

(23 weeks)

MONDAY.

Tucker calls me at the office.

"What are you doing?" he asks.

"Working," I say.

"No, really," he says.

In truth, Tucker's call finds me washing an apple over my wastepaper basket with coffee from my mug.

I hang up, telling him I have to get back to work, but instead I sit at my desk trying to decide what to order for lunch. I know I should have a salad but I want to have smoked meat. Either way, I should probably stop eating at my desk. My computer keyboard is starting to look like the floor of a bus station washroom. To get the dirt out from between the keys, I turn it upside down and tap it against my desk. In so doing, I inadvertently Google "IMYH." One of the first results is a Sheryl Crow fan site—IMYH being the acronym for her song "If It Makes You Happy."

I take this as a sign to have smoked meat.

THURSDAY.

I take Howard out to his favourite steakhouse for a belated birthday dinner. While some men pride themselves on marksmanship, yachtsmanship, or even penmanship, Howard prides himself on steaksmanship—the ability to eat vast quantities of steak. He orders the largest one on the menu and I do the same.

Everything is so rich and heavy. Even the salad seems soaked in a dressing made of mercury. While waiting for the steak, we chomp away at handfuls of bacon bits like they're peanuts.

During the meal I try to match Howard, eating whatever he does. Across the table, he stares at me over a steak bone practically gnawed down to the marrow. His eyes are narrowed, as though sizing up an opponent.

"I see what you're doing," he says. "You're trying to go toe to toe with the kid."

"I'm trying to enjoy a meal," I lie, my stomach beginning to ache.

After our dinner, we each eat a wafer-thin chocolate that comes with the cheque. I feel mine go down like an iron barbell plate.

I leave the restaurant, woozy, my stomach doing flip flops.

"I think I might have steak poisoning," I finally admit, a sob in my voice.

"If anything, you may have pork poisoning," Howard says. "You ate about an industrial dumpster's worth of bacon."

I beg him to stop saying "bacon" and "dumpster" because the words are making me feel like my stomach is a plummeting elevator full of oatmeal.

In what I know is Howard's version of a victory lap, he suggests we stop on the way home for ice cream. To refuse would be to admit defeat.

"If it makes you happy," I say, my face shiny with sweat. And moments later, at the ice cream parlour, as Howard eats a double scoop of pistachio and I force-feed myself a ball of orange sherbet, it would seem it truly does.

FRIDAY.

Gregor visits me at my office.

"What's this?" he asks, pointing to the large yoga ball under my desk.

"Someone in the office was throwing it out and I thought I'd try sitting on it while working. It's supposed to do wonders for the posture. Want to try sitting on it?"

"I wouldn't even touch it," he says. "Balls are great for dribbling, kicking, and helping man determine winning lotto numbers, but not for sitting on. A yoga ball is the rare object that can boast having had buttocks pressed against every millimetre of its surface. The sphere, my friend. Nature's perfect cootie catcher."

I guess that's why it's the perfect shape for a place that's home to asses like us.

The Weight of Worry
(22 weeks)

MONDAY.

My office chair has been sinking of its own accord. Maintenance has been by to fix the problem twice and they still can't seem to figure out what's going on. In my heart I fear I know something that maintenance does not: the chair responds to emotional heaviness, and confronted with seven hundred pounds of worry, it doesn't stand a chance.

WEDNESDAY.

I'm at the airport with Gregor. We're flying to Toronto for a mutual friend's wedding on Saturday. In line at the gate, we watch as people late for their flight are rushed to the front of the line.

"I don't get it," Gregor says. "These guys roll out of

bed fifteen minutes before their plane's about to take off, and they're treated like members of the landed gentry. It's airport welfare!"

Walking through security, my bag accidentally wheels over Gregor's loafer, scuffing it.

"Sorry," I say.

"There's an old Russian expression," he says, bending over to rub his shoe, "an apology isn't a fur coat."

"Of course it isn't," I say. "One's an abstract idea and the other's a physical object."

"Boy, you're a barrel of laughs," he says. "By your logic, 'who's on first' should have been called 'the exchange in which a personal pronoun is confused with a proper name.'"

Boarding for our plane is announced. We stand and wait as the people in first class have their tickets taken.

"I don't get it," Gregor says. "These guys just roll in making more in a week than I do in a year and they get treated like members of the landed gentry!"

"Call it airport corporate welfare," I say.

On the flight, Gregor forces me to take the middle seat.

The stewardess comes by with the snack wagon.

"Cookies or Bits & Bites?" she asks.

"The latter," I say.

"Sorry?" she says.

"The one that isn't the cookies," I say.

The stewardess leaves and Gregor turns to me.

"God forbid you should stoop to say Bits & Bites."

"My grip on my dignity is tenuous." Which is why it's important for me to at least maintain a grip on my armrest. At the moment, though, it feels as though the man to my right is trying his best to subtly elbow me off. He and I stare straight ahead, pretending to be entranced by our newspapers, but all the while, we both know that we are locked in battle.

I turn to my left to explain the situation to Gregor so that he knows, too.

"There's an unwritten rule that the man in the middle has claim to the armrests," I say.

"Unwritten where?" he asks. "On an asylum wall? What hope is there of peace in the Middle East if two strangers eating airplane snacks can't even share a two-inch slat of plastic?"

Of course Gregor is right. I lift my elbow off the armrest and, almost immediately, I start to feel better about myself. The feeling, though, is short-lived, as to my left, Gregor shoves my elbow off our armrest, spilling Bits & Bites all over my lap.

"Sorry," he says.

SUNDAY.

Gregor stays an extra day, and I fly back alone. The plane is going through turbulence, and every time there's a big bump I look over at the stewardess and study her face. I am looking for a wide-toothed grin. Nothing clenched or strained. Nothing that says, "What the heck was that?" For me, perhaps even more important than bringing me bourbon, these smiles are a stewardess's most important responsibility. In such moments it feels as though it is these easy smiles that keep the plane, as well as life itself, afloat. At work on Monday, before sitting down on my office chair, I'll empty my heart of all worry, if only for a moment, and see what happens.

The Writer's Life

(21 weeks)

MONDAY.

Incapable of writing the monologue for this week's radio show, I head to the CBC cafeteria. There's a self-serve fruit salad bar, and I've gotten into the habit of seeing how much fruit I can cram into the little containers they give you. It's a bit like a game of Tetris. As I walk back to my desk I imagine pitching the cup against the wall and watching it explode. A Molotov fruit cocktail. Packing the fruit cup proves to be the most productive part of my day.

TUESDAY.

Still in need of inspiration, I set out for the Dollar Cinema to watch *He's Just Not That Into You*. When I get there, though, I learn there was an error in the ad, and the theatre's been rented out to a Sri Lankan community group for the evening. But since I'm already there and in the mood for popcorn, I stay for the screening.

It's a romantic comedy and, although not subtitled, I do a decent job of following along—until the moment when the male lead, for no apparent reason, leaps off a balcony and graphically splits his head open. When he reappears in the film's closing credits, dancing, I decide that the death might have been a dream. Or perhaps the credits are a dream. Narratively speaking, Sri Lankan cinema is more complicated than *Finnegans Wake*.

On my way home, trying to make heads or tails of the movie, I cross paths with a skunk. It sees me and stops. We stand there, face to face.

I can't think of a single person I know, in the last twenty-five years, who's been sprayed by a skunk. Maybe it was the kind of thing that was bigger in the seventies—something that went out with the hula hoop or sitting backwards on kitchen chairs. Back in those heady days, everyone was bathing in tomato juice while listening to the Doobie Brothers, but in recent years, it seems as though our two species have reached some kind of armistice.

A part of me wants to be sprayed, like I want proof of an urban legend—if not an excuse to avoid writing my monologue. We stare at each other. We wait. Finally, the skunk runs under a balcony. I find myself feeling oddly rejected.

THURSDAY.

I've been working from home. I've told myself I wouldn't leave the apartment until I've finished my monologue. It's been three days now and my supply of martini olives is running dangerously low.

I allow myself to step onto the porch to check the mail, and I find a postcard from Starlee. It's of an elephant swimming underwater, using its nose as a snorkel. I pin it to the wall above my desk. I can't help thinking that the elephant looks like he's smiling, like he's pleasantly surprised to have stepped into an impossible world where he is as light as smoke. Perhaps he is willing himself to believe that he'll never have to leave, that he can live among the fish for as long as he likes. Somewhere deep down, though, he must know that eventually he'll have to leave. I am not unlike that elephant, content to abandon elephanthood— until the olives run out.

As I walk to the grocery store in the drizzling rain, I catch sight of myself in a store window. I look like a live-action version of Pig Pen from *Peanuts*. This is confirmed by two pamphleteering Greenpeace workers who allow me to walk past them without a word.

Back at home, I spend the evening alternately staring at the computer screen and the rain outside the window. At about 11:00 p.m., I hear a knock at the door. It's Tucker.

"New shirt?" he asks, walking into my apartment. "The blue really brings out the despair in your eyes."

"You smell like pizza," I say.

"Thanks," he says. It turns out he's brought some over for me.

At the end of *Save the Tiger*, Jack Lemmon, who in 1973 was already playing sad old men, says that he just wants the girl from the Cole Porter song, someone who can walk all night in the rain and still smell of perfume. If the smell of pizza is a kind of perfume—and I would argue that it is, or at the very least better than skunk—I guess I've found the girl from the song. Sadly, but maybe not so sadly, it's Tucker. And if he keeps up with the pizza delivery, I should be able to maintain the lifestyle of the shut-in artist that I've grown accustomed to.

PICASSO GOLDSTEIN

July 29, 1912

It has been days since I've produced any art or left my studio. My assistant, Claude, passes me food under the door, and as a result I eat mostly sliced meats, thinly cut cheeses, and flattened baguettes which often bear the stamp of Claude's boot heel. In return, I slide him out coins. I peer under the door and see his greedy fingers pry them off the floorboards like spiders eating flies.

I cannot leave my studio because to leave would mean opening the door, and opening the door, even for a moment, would mean allowing Picasso to slip in and set his thieving eyes upon my art. I've come to believe he's not a painter at all, but a pickpocket and a shape-shifter. I must hide myself from his gaze lest he steal my very soul!

Since banning Picasso from my atelier he has become fiendishly inventive and as agile as a howler monkey. At night I see him in the shadows, creeping along the sill outside my window. Several days after blanketing over the glass with newspaper, word reached me through Claude that the Evil Genius had begun making collages. Out of what, you ask? Why, newspaper, of course. I give him nothing and still he takes.

August 3

The sick, sad, twisted irony of it all is that my name, too, is Picasso. Picasso Goldstein. It is a childhood nickname. I was originally named Pegasus by my father, a scholar of ancient Greek, but my brother Maurice, a blowfish-brained imbecile, could never pronounce Pegasus and when he tried it sounded like "Pegabo," which my grandmother, a shrewish, near-deaf nitpicker, heard as Peccadillo. Once the census-taker, an illiterate alcoholic slob, arrived at our door, my fate was sealed. "Picasso" was the name he scrawled across his clipboard. And that, as they say, was that.

Sharing the evil bandit's name has not been easy. When introduced in society as Picasso the painter I am met by glazed-over looks.

"I am not *that* Picasso," I say, my lower lip trembling and my upper lip sweaty.

Picasso has stolen my best ideas. He has stolen my patrons—who have included marquises, counts, viscounts, barons, and one British Columbian prince; he has stolen my galleries, my women, and my friends. He has even stolen my very name. He has left me with nothing.

August 12

Some back story so you do not think me completely mad: The thievery all began in the summer of 1901 when a young Pablo Picasso was brought to my studio by a mutual acquaintance, a Madame Voillard, who carried about a curly lap dog.

"Pablo is an artist, too," Madame Voillard said, introducing us.

I showed the balding little homunculus kindness, patting his head and encouraging him in his hobby.

"What's this?" he asked, gesturing towards a large painting of a nude. It was made entirely from various shades of blue.

"It's a naked woman," I said, pinching his Buddha-like belly good-naturedly. "Never seen one of those, eh?"

"But it's all in blue," he said.

"I was too lazy to get up from my stool and fetch other colours," I said.

It was several months after Picasso left my studio that I saw in *Le Journal* a rave review of his new show. It featured works of his "Blue Period," as it would later be called. I went to bed that night gnashing my teeth.

I feel Picasso out there, his horrible eyes which see through studio walls! His alien brain which is psychic and robs me of my ideas at the moment of their conception! But I remain steadfast, thinking nothing, saying nothing, looking at nothing. I keep my mind as blank as my canvases, for as soon as I create, he appropriates, turning what is starkly— boldly—original into a facsimile! The genius of his theft is how he leaves in his wake the crown of banditry upon *my* head! To be forever perceived as the thief of my own work!

August 19

Yesterday, waking up with the fires of creativity burning, I felt the need to paint, and so I undertook some tiny watercolours—no more than the size of cufflink buttons. In this way, I reasoned, I could hunch over them, protecting them from invisible eyes.

I set upon my subject from memory: my childhood violin instructor—a taciturn, ungenerous Aunt Doris type with the perennial expression of a perplexed bonobo. With careful, teeny brushstrokes I captured the upturned slant of her horrid smile, and for the first time in weeks I managed a smile of my own. Sweet, sweet art!

It was only as I poured the excess coloured water down the drain that a cold shudder ran through me. I imagined Picasso down there in the pipes, licking his chops like a sewer rat, a pan lifted above his head to catch the dripping of my brushes, readying himself to run home and, in his alchemist's laboratory, separate the black water into colours—my colours! To decode my tints, my half tints, and—the thieving guttersnipe—my quarter tints!

Never! I crushed the tiny masterpiece with my thumb and drank the remaining paint water. I then vowed never to paint again—not until I knew with certainty that France was rid of Picasso.

September 1

Claude tells me that Picasso has exhibited a painting called *Les Demoiselles d'Avignon*. He slipped a shoddy sketch of the abomination under my studio door in his pudgy idiot's hand. Even with his crude, caveman-like draftsmanship I could see what it was: a blatant rip-off of my drawing *Les Putains Malades*, a study of herpes sores I'd drawn for a medical textbook last year. The composition! The poses! It was all my work, ingested and regurgitated. On my hands and knees, I screamed under the door crack that Picasso was the devil.

"And so, Claude, are you!" I shrieked. *"Tête dure! Salop!* Swine!"

September 7

Claude has been starving me out. He has slipped neither meat nor cheese under my door in several days. I know that he now works for Picasso. From the day I met him, I knew Claude was not to be trusted. At this moment I wish nothing more than to be able to pluck my dandy stick from the umbrella stand and beat the back of his calves a cerise red as I did in better days. I know that I am now truly alone.

September 15

I am done with painting. It, along with Picasso, has destroyed my life. I have spent the day in a rage, breaking my paintbrushes into tiny pieces and flinging paint against the walls and unused canvases of my studio. Everything is a mess of drippings and splatter. At long last I am satisfied for I have created chaos, and the beauty of chaos is that it can't ever be stolen. The agency is sending over a new assistant tomorrow. A prematurely bald drunkard by the name of Pollock. I'll let him deal with the mess.

A Still Shark Is Still a Shark
(20 weeks)

SUNDAY.

In my parents' living room, my father reads a book on the couch beside me while my mother exercises in the other room. We are having a visit.

"Two hundred twenty-five," my mother calls from her bedroom. She's been giving my father and me an update on the calories she's burned riding her exercise bike.

"She's cycling herself into non-existence," my father says, getting up from the couch to use the washroom. He's gone for twenty calories, and when he returns, he is distraught.

"Instead of sitting down on the toilet seat," he says, "I sat on the closed lid. Did you close the toilet?"

I confess that I did, and my father is outraged.

"This has never been a closed-toilet-lid family," he says.

"I really feel part of a rich tradition," I say.

I explain that closing the toilet lid is something I started doing after reading an article in a science journal about the molecules of toilet water that escape with each flush.

"Your toothbrush might as well be a toilet brush," I say.

"Two hundred forty-five," my mother says.

"This place is a nuthouse." My father picks his book back up, and we continue our visit in an easy silence that will be broken only by the next chime of calories.

MONDAY.

Five hundred. According to the McDonald's website, there are five hundred calories in a McRib, half of which are from fat.

I'm studying up on my prey in anticipation of dining out with Josh. Though I have never eaten one, the McRib is a sandwich that's fascinated me for years. For one thing, if it's popular, why not keep it on the regular menu? And if it isn't, why keep bringing it back every few years? Either people want it or they don't.

On the drive to McDonald's, Josh explains his theory.

"The McRib is fleeting, and its ephemerality stirs anxiety in the hearts of men. Any day one might walk into McDonald's and the McRib will no longer be there. One must seize it before it is driven back into oblivion. It's like the green Shamrock Shake, but without the stabilizing tie-in of a St. Patrick's Day."

"Maybe the McRib could be tied in to national heart disease awareness week."

Josh thinks that might be the stupidest thing he's ever heard. We argue the point passionately.

Another point of fascination is that the McRib is composed of meat that's been shaped into the form of rib bones. In terms of its immanence and use of self-guise as disguise, the McRib is probably the most postmodern item on the McDonald's menu.

At the restaurant, the cashier tells us that they stopped serving the McRib a day earlier.

We are both a little crushed.

On our way to Chinatown for dumplings, we cheer our spirits by rolling down the windows and arguing over the difference between dumplings and kreplach. We do so intensely enough to make passersby stop and stare.

THURSDAY.

While watching a documentary about sharks, I become saddened that sharks don't seem to be scaring me the way they used to. When I was a kid, about eighty percent of my time was spent worrying about being eaten by sharks. This was during the seventies, and with all the movies—*Shark!*, *Jaws*, *Jaws 2*, and *Jaws 3* in 3D—everyone was. Going to the beach was an act of daredevilhood. I remember dropping a hard-boiled egg into the surf to see if a shark would come and get it—to see if it was safe to swim—and my dad yelling to never mind the shark, he was going to murder me for wasting eggs.

But nowadays, or at least on some days, being eaten by a shark doesn't seem so bad. I mean, it would be bad, but after the first couple bites, I suspect no worse than missing out on McRib season or listening to someone talk about their RRSP contribution.

I've financial matters on my mind this evening because I've promised myself, despite its being a major anxiety, to get a head start on my taxes. But instead, I continue to watch the documentary on sharks, nostalgic for old fears and still unwilling to confront new ones.

A Place to Hang One's Cape
(19 weeks)

While reading *The New Yorker,* I tear out a poem and slip it into my wallet. It's where I keep the things most dear to me, but as I keep my wallet in my back pocket, I must be economical in my curating, for too much dearness will damage my spine. The rump of a Greek god is one thing; the rump of a centaur is another.

I get up to go to the bathroom when I realize that my bathroom door hasn't been able to shut all the way in God knows how long. I guess I've been living alone too long. Maybe someday I'll become the kind of classy older bachelor who's comfortable buying himself flowers on the way home from work—a man who takes calèche rides through the park with his poodle while sipping cognac from a flask. In this scenario, I'm seeing a cape featured prominently. And an apartment suited to my station in life—with doors that close and hooks to hang one's capes.

SATURDAY.

I turn on my computer to search Craigslist for apartment listings. The wireless window pops up, and I realize with some regret that all I know about my neighbours is their wireless network names: Krypton, Space Balls, Couscous, and Scarlet. From this I can tell little else than that they're fans of Superman, Mel Brooks, Middle Eastern cuisine, and the colour red. I look out my window, wondering whose house is whose and what private food and entertainment consumption occurs in each and how I will never get to know.

SUNDAY.

Gregor comes over to help with my apartment search.

"I'm thrilled about this move," he says. "I intend to keep monetizing you long after you're dead, so we need a place people can continue to come visit and celebrate your memory—a Canadian Graceland where European tourists can say, 'It's so much smaller and stinkier than I imagined.' As your manager/real estate agent, I'll find you a proper home by nightfall."

"Nightfall?"

"We Ehrlichs are a persistent bunch. My uncle Perry

Ehrlich, armed with only a dessert spoon, was said to have once chased a canned peach all around the bowl, across the length of the table, and along the waxed pine floor of the dining room. He eventually trapped the renegade fruit slice two hours later under a basement armoire."

"And then what? Did he eat it?"

"I believe he had a stroke."

"That would make some canned peach commercial."

MONDAY.

With Gregor having turned up nothing but a refurbished school bus and a ten thousand square foot loft in Chelsea, New York, I pick up a newspaper to comb the classifieds, old-school. When I return home I find Boosh on the kitchen table. It appears she has eaten half my flowers.

She gives me a meaningful, almost soulful, look.

If only Boosh knew a few words. I'm not saying enough to explain her obsession with squirrels, or the meaning behind her howls when the theme to *As It Happens* comes on the radio, but a couple of words. "Good morning." "What's up?" "Nice to be sitting here with you."

I return her look, gazing at her searchingly, looking for answers—if not for where to live, maybe just what to have as a mid-afternoon snack.

"Canned peaches," I imagine her saying. "Use a fork."

Medium Is the Message

(18 weeks)

TUESDAY.

I'm on the phone with Tony.

"Ever feel slightly off?" he asks. "But only slightly. Like your T-shirt's on backwards or something."

"I often wear my T-shirts backwards on purpose," I say. "It makes me feel like with each step I'm travelling back into the past. Ah, the past! That's where regrets are born."

"Plus with the tag in front, you can dip your head under the collar and contemplate your own mediumness."

"Speaking of being medium," I say, "I recently read that in experiments involving cockroaches and aggression, it turns out that aggressiveness is a quality most valuable in medium-sized cockroaches. Evidently, this is because they have the most to lose."

"What can a cockroach possibly have to lose?" he asks.

At this, we conclude our conversation. Having achieved a difficult Zen koan, what is there left to say?

WEDNESDAY.

Howard calls up to see if I want to go out for seafood.

"One of my goals this year is to eat more lobster," he says. "And wait until you see me in a lobster bib. It's a very handsome, slimming look. Well worth your paying for dinner just to behold me in it."

"When you were ten," I ask, "did you ever think you'd one day be in your thirties hustling lobster?"

"If, at ten, I'd gone to a palm reader who told me I'd one day be living in a cardboard box, subsisting on gobstoppers, and able to watch *The Twilight Zone* five days a week on cable, I'd think the future was looking pretty good."

"Can we blame our public school education for breeding in us such lowered expectations?" I ask. "Maybe we'd have made more of ourselves if we were home schooled."

"Depends which home the schooling was taking place in," he says. "In my home, our encyclopedias were used to prop up windows. My dad kept the whole set in a cardboard box in the garage beside his tool box."

"How does fish and chips sound?" I ask.

"Pretty good," he says.

Never underestimate the power of medium expectations.

As Elusive as a Peach Slice
(17 weeks)

SUNDAY.

I'm sitting on the couch playing video games with Tucker. As he plays, he tells me about a conversation he had in a bar the night before with a woman who was taller than him.

"It's not that I'm short," Tucker told her. "It's just that I'm far away."

It's my turn to play, and Tucker watches the screen.

"Even as a Pac-Man, your personality really comes across," he says. "The way you run away from things while still pausing to look back."

"I guess I always try to make time for regret," I say. "I wonder if the ghosts are Pac-Men who've died in games past."

He hands me another beer. The more I drink, the less afraid I become of getting caught by ghosts, but the more attractive a nap starts to feel. In sleep things are simpler.

No regret over the past. No worry for the future. Only the present. And as bad as a dream gets, at least you get to sleep through it.

MONDAY.

In the dream, I am able to fly. I haven't had a dream like this since I was a kid. The only problem is that I'm only able to fly half a foot above the ground. Also, I can only fly about a quarter of a mile an hour. Still, I am flying. I head to Montreal's Olympic Stadium, but after several minutes of tedious, unspectacular flight, I decide that it'd be faster just to take the metro. With this thought, I am suddenly awake.

FRIDAY.

After a large, tasty Chinese meal, I lean back and decide to just enjoy the moment.

"What's the matter?" Tony asks.

"Nothing," I say. "Why?"

"You suddenly look like Charles Manson trying to remember where he parked."

"I was trying to be in the moment," I say, angrily and no longer in the moment. "This is why I can't relax—because whenever I do, I end up looking like an antisocial lunatic."

When I'm finished my whining, I realize I'm still hungry. I've been trying to watch myself, and so I debate whether to top things off with a fortune cookie.

"You just ate three egg rolls and a family-sized plate of General Tao chicken," Tony says. "Go for gold."

I crack it open and read the fortune. "Spoil yourself a little."

And so I decide to eat half. And as I continue to eat the other half, I'm not exactly in the moment, but somewhere adjacent to it.

Timing

(16 weeks)

SUNDAY, 10:30 A.M.

Marie-Claude calls to invite me over for dinner. A five o'clock dinner.

"What're you, on Honolulu time?"

"It's called having children," she says.

"Are your children in their seventies? Eating dinner this early takes planning—lead time. I need to retool my whole digestive clock. I'd have been getting up at 4:00 a.m. for the past two weeks if I'd known."

"Go out and paint a fence," she says. "Work up a healthy appetite."

"When was the last time you heard someone tell a grown man to 'work up a healthy appetite'? In this day and age, it's just not done!"

1:30 P.M.

In an attempt to work up a healthy appetite, I nap on the couch while watching TV. Boxing is on and it's making me nostalgic. As a child I watched the sport with my father while punching the couch cushions. I was a cocky kid and thought that if Muhammad Ali agreed to fight me on his knees, I might have a chance.

I wanted my father to think of me as a hero of some kind. Little did I know that, as far as he was concerned, my single greatest act of heroism would only arrive in my thirties, upon losing my wallet in a Chicago taxicab and continuing to lead a relatively normal life.

"You handled that courageously," he'd repeat whenever the story arose. "After something like that, they'd have had to put me away for good."

During a commercial, I head to the kitchen and stare at a shelf full of cereal boxes, uncertain as to whether I should be having lunch or a pre-dinner snack. Cereal as a snack means throwing in marshmallows, while cereal for lunch means slicing in a pear.

If the early dinner was a sporting event, I guess this would be like some kind of warm-up.

5:30 P.M.

After dinner, I sit on Marie-Claude's couch, depressed. So much of my time is spent thinking about what I'm going to eat next that, with dinner behind me so early in the evening, I've nothing left to look forward to.

7:30 P.M.

At home, I try to calculate how much of my day is taken up with thoughts of food. If you were to break down my thoughts on a pie chart (and what other chart could possibly be more suited to the task?) it would look like this: 30 percent on what my next meal will be; 10 percent on who'll show up at my funeral; 10 percent on sexual fantasies; 20 percent on revenge fantasies; 15 percent on what I should've said to various security guards and receptionists in verbal altercations from decades past; and 10 percent on hair loss. This leaves me with 5 percent for contemplating the "big picture" stuff like what movies I'm going to see next.

9:15 P.M.

Against all probability, I find myself heroically peckish. Perhaps there is an upside to eating early, after all: looking forward to your second dinner.

I decide to go out for a sub and, as usual, I order the twelve-incher. My intention is always the same: to eat half and save the other half for tomorrow's lunch. But I always blow it by eating the whole thing. I know that if I can just wait ten minutes after that first six inches, I can pull it off. But they are a very hard ten minutes.

I attempt to ride them out by looking away from the sandwich and out the window of the restaurant. I ruminate on sandwiches past: the time I bit my tongue while eating a meatball sub; the open-faced tuna salad sandwich I once sat on at a shiva house.

After five minutes of these reminiscences, I look down at the last half, pick it up, and bite into it. I feel that somehow, over the course of my life, I've earned it, and, as always, it proves just as good as the first.

Stuff
(15 weeks)

WEDNESDAY.

After weeks of searching, it's now only a few days until moving day, and I've decided to spend the afternoon packing—though by "packing" I mean deliberating over what to pack and what to leave behind.

Like my parents, my inclination is to save. I've even decided to store an ex-girlfriend's mother's social work master's thesis archived on 5¼-inch floppy disks. The thesis somehow made its way into my possession, and so I continue to feel a responsibility for it.

Likewise, after schlepping around *War and Peace* from apartment to apartment for twenty years without making any headway with it, I still can't bring myself to toss it. No matter how unlikely, it's still possible that one day I might conquer it. As the psychotherapist Irvin Yalom writes, death is the impossibility of possibility. And so holding on to the book feels like a vote in favour of all that's still possible.

I look out my apartment window and see that the box of books and clothing I left out there with a "free" sign remains untouched. I feel like my erudition and fashion sense have been roundly rejected—albeit by complete strangers.

"I am not my books and I am not my clothes," I tell myself as I draw the curtains closed, pull the curtains off the wall, and pack them into a box. I place the box on the curb and watch them get passed over by strangers.

"If I'm not my curtains," I think anxiously, "then what in the world am I?"

A few moments later, the doorbell rings. It's Tucker.

"I literally can't give away my belongings," I say, staring out the uncurtained window. "No one's even taking my red checkered shirt, the one you said made me look like a picnic table. Just think, if you took it you could lie down on the floor while wearing it and eat a bowl of potato salad off your chest, the whole meal feeling al fresco."

"What's the sense in moving this?" he asks, pulling out an almost empty bottle of single malt scotch.

"It's got about two shots left," I say, "and I've been saving it for a special occasion."

"I got news for you," he says, uncorking the bottle, "that occasion has come."

Tucker swigs some scotch, hands it back to me, and offers to run down to the store and pick up some cigars.

In the silence after his exit, I survey my place, taking in all the boxes containing my belongings. It occurs to me that life isn't just about the accumulation and curating of stuff. It's also about letting stuff go.

FRIDAY.

Today at the CBC, I notice they've created a new, well-lit display case for the Oscar an employee won for best animated short in 1982. I recently learned that there's an old Hollywood legend that if you touch an Oscar, you'll never win an Oscar. I wonder if the employee who put it in the case knew this and whether he felt conflicted.

"You're forty-five," he might have said to himself, "and you've yet to discover any latent cinematic talent; still, to pick up the trophy means relinquishing all childish hope."

At a certain point, adulthood becomes a numbers game. Odds are you're never going win an Oscar, bowl a perfect game, finish *War and Peace*, or, in most cases, even learn how to drive if you haven't already learned by the age of eighteen. At thirty-nine, I'm beginning to see that middle age might mean having more failures behind you than triumphs ahead. So you might as well just polish the other guy's trophy and put it in the display case. The lucky ones have a scotch bottle with a couple shots left for when they get home.

Inbetweenness

(14 weeks)

SUNDAY.

I've just finished moving all my stuff into the new apartment, and deciding where to put certain personal effects is proving difficult. Where to place the empty box of Reese's Pieces that contains a doodle I'm rather fond of? In my old apartment, it just sat under the couch. Or what to do with the sunglass lenses that, years earlier, became detached from their frames—frames I'm still hopeful will one day resurface?

But I am enjoying the feeling of inbetweenness—that not-yet-being-settled feeling—and I plan on dragging it out as long as I can, because it's a state of grace where all things are permissible. For instance, this evening I ate takeout pizza off a cardboard box while drinking wine from a soup pot (like a cowboy!), and I watched the TV on the floor beside me, inches from my face (like being at the drive-in!).

I think I may have stumbled upon a new school of interior design.

TUESDAY.

Marie-Claude and her daughters babysat Howard's pugs, Desmond and Bruce, over the weekend. Marie-Claude calls up to let me know how it went.

"The girls want Bruce to be their godfather," she says.

"But I'm their godfather," I say.

"Lucky for you it isn't an electable position."

"A godfather's job is to supply moral tutelage," I say, defensively.

"Bruce licks their feet," she says.

Not to lose the upper hand, I offer to pick up the girls for lunch. What taking a nine- and seven-year-old out for hamburgers lacks in the laughing-at-your-jokes department is more than made up for in the leaving-you-plenty-of-leftovers-to-eat department.

After a hardy meal, I drop them back home and, after kissing them goodbye, press a small gift into their hands.

"A sunglass monocle," I say, "for each of you."

WEDNESDAY.

Tony knocks on my door, wanting me to join him for souvlaki. I tell him I've too much to get done in my new place. I show him the to-do list.

"You deserve a break," he says, looking it over. "You've got half your items ticked off."

"Yes," I say, "but vacuuming, dusting—I did those things before making the list. I only wrote them down for the pleasure of ticking them off."

Sometimes I write down "do the dishes" as "wash cups, wash cutlery, wash plates" just for the extra ticks.

"Give me that list," Tony says. He pulls out his pen, writes something down, and hands it back to me.

Eat souvlaki.

Who can argue with a written commandment? I grab my coat and get ready to eat souvlaki. It will prove the most satisfying tick of the day.

THURSDAY.

I wake up out of a dream in which Tucker makes a cameo as a raisin in my porridge.

"What business is it of yours to dream about me?" he asks when I call up to tell him about it.

"I have no control over what I dream," I say. "And why would you care anyway?"

"I've had occasion to glimpse the things that go on in your mind," he says, "so the idea of spending any time there is upsetting."

I change the subject by asking if he'd like my inflatable Bozo punching bag. It's one of those dolls that, when you hit it, it pops right back up; but since I never got around to filling the base with sand, whenever I punch it, it stays down.

"I had one of those when I was a kid," Tucker says. "Playing with it helped nurture my budding sense of futility."

He agrees to take it, believing the defective version that stays down might give him the sense of accomplishment he's always craved. I ask if perhaps coming over and helping unpack my boxes might also afford him a sense of accomplishment, but he declines.

The truth is, I'm pretty happy to keep living out of boxes anyway. The opportunity to live like a hobo in your own home doesn't come along that often, so it might be nice to stretch it out for a couple more days. Maybe a week. A month, tops.

Perfect Imperfection
(13 weeks)

MONDAY.

In the midst of showering, I realize I've been using the same bar of soap for about a month now. From this I conclude that I am either a) in the midst of a Hanukkah-type miracle; or b) simply not scrubbing hard enough. There have been many failures in my life. Now I can add "showering" to the portfolio.

I grind the soap into my flesh with vigour—to try and catch up. I am working towards something far greater than mere cleanliness. I am rubbing out an opponent. This is some serious *Old Man and the Sea* kind of stuff.

"You have been a worthy adversary, but annihilate you I must."

An hour and fifteen minutes later, I emerge from the shower. I am late for work, shrivelled like a raisin, but feeling triumphant.

TUESDAY.

I buy a new couch for my new place. My mother is insistent that I get arm covers for it.

"Why?" I ask.

"You'd be surprised by how quickly arms can rub out," she says.

"How quickly?" I ask.

"Well, it takes twenty, thirty years," she says, "but it happens, and when it does, you'll be sorry."

"I won't be sorry," I say. "I'll feel a sense of accomplishment." By way of explanation, I tell her about the bar of soap from the day before and how grinding it into nothingness through determination and perseverance was very rewarding.

"Who taught me how to shower anyway?" I ask. "Because I don't think I've been doing it right."

My mother looks at me, glassy-eyed.

Persian rug makers are said to leave in one mistake on purpose. In this way, they can look upon their creation and be reminded that all things made by man are imperfect. Yet this is what makes their work more valuable than if it had been made by machine. Persian rugs bespeak their maker's humanity just as my imperfections bespeak my mother's humanity. Hers is an extreme humanity, for if I were a carpet, I would be possessed of more than one mistake. I would be a knotted, unravelling carpet full of cigarette burns and grape juice stains.

SUNDAY.

It's Mother's Day, my nephew's first, and when I get to the Greek restaurant my family is already at the table.

We focus all our attention on the baby. We constantly worry for his comfort and safety, and so every time he shifts in his baby seat, we clutch our hearts and mop the sweat from our brows with fistfuls of napkin.

"I love him so much it hurts," my sister says, her hand on her mouth.

"Me too," my father says. "It physically hurts."

"It's like someone is beating me with sandbags," my mother says.

"With me it's more of a stabbing," my father counters.

"I love him so much," my aunt says, "it's like having a serrated blade corkscrewed into my side."

Not one to be outdone, my sister weighs in again: "I love him so much I feel like I'm drowning in love and can't breathe." She demonstrates the sensation by making gagging and gasping noises while scratching at the air.

As we eat, my father accidentally tips a plate of olive oil onto his lap. Pretty soon afterwards, my aunt somehow manages to drip the wax from the candelabra onto her pants, and when I look over at my mother, she is wearing a bib of smeared tzatziki sauce across the chest of her black turtleneck.

Ironically, the baby proves to be the neatest eater of us all. Truly, it feels like he is the best of us all. I look over at him and he smiles a little smile at me that fills my heart with so much love … it's as though I have had my eyes sprayed with mace and my heart stabbed with a salad fork. Wincing, I reach across the table for another soothing spoonful of taramasalata, and as I do, I drag my jacket sleeve through a puddle of spilled gravy. It feels like the final brush stroke to a happy family portrait.

Beating God to the Punch
(12 weeks)

SUNDAY.

In celebration of spring, I've shaved my head again.

After work, I meet up with Gregor for a drink.

"Again with the shaved head," he cries at the sight of me. "You used to have funny hair—hair that a person could laugh at. You might as well kiss your comedy career goodbye."

"First of all," I say, "I'm not a comedian. I'm a humorist."

"What's the difference?"

"A humorist is a comedian who doesn't necessarily make you laugh."

"Well, anyone who is even adjacent to the comedy biz, be it rodeo clown or wise-cracking waitress, needs to look funny."

"Come on," I say. "I've just traded the wild wispy locks of a Larry Fine for the clean-shaven dome of a Curly

Howard. What I'm saying is I'm still a stooge. Plus, this way, I don't have to worry about going bald, because I've beaten God to the punch."

Gregor shakes his head.

"That's like being a bread that advertises itself as already stale so you don't have to worry about it going bad."

My balding began in grade eight. I was the only kid in junior high who was already sporting a comb-over by the age of twelve. Now when I see young guys, still teenagers, walking around with thinning hair, I just want to gather them up in my arms like fallen comrades. I'd tell them "it gets better" but that would be a lie as it only gets worse. Except in the case of Bruce Willis. And George Foreman.

On the one hand, losing your hair happens so slowly that it allows you to adjust. That's a kindness on nature's part. (And what with the lions eating gazelles, the tsunamis, and such, nature's not always the nicest.) But in other ways, the slowness is part of the painful absurdity. It's like being gradually ladled in a hot sticky cherry sauce of baldness. You feel it coming down but, like one of those nightmares where you're immobilized, you just stay there, taking it.

As a child, I always wanted to succeed, get somewhere in life—but I wanted to do it with my hair. To do so bald seemed pointless. As one's baldness blossoms, so too does a kind of low-grade nihilism. And I should say that a greater indignity than merely going bald was going bald in the manner known in bald circles as "The Friar Tuck." This is when you maintain the wisps at the front—those brave, stupid soldiers who maintain their post in the front ranks, never having learned that the war's been lost and the officers in the back have all gone home.

Oh sure, now that I'm an adult, I could get myself a wig—something blond and floppy like Alexander Godunov's mane. But with friends like mine, it'd end up torn from my skull and hackysacked about the room. Of course I could move to a new city and start over, but it takes so long for me to make new friends. Even terrible ones.

THURSDAY.

I'm halfway through the new Philip Roth book. My progress is slow, because every couple paragraphs I turn back to the author's photo on the jacket. Roth's right eye looks so much like my father's that I can't stop examining it. Everyone has one eye that looks kinder than the other and Roth's kind eye is his right. I have noted in photos that my father's kind eye is his left, but even his right eye is kinder than Roth's right. If I were Philip Roth I would consider an eye patch. I'm sure he's the kind of man whose friends wouldn't dare tear it off.

To the Bottom!

(11 weeks)

SUNDAY.

I've recently taken up running and have been trying to figure out a route that would allow me to run nearly all the way downhill, while never having to actually go uphill. Short of living in an M.C. Escher drawing, though, I fear this might be an impossible undertaking. Running downhill reminds you of what a powerful force gravity actually is. If only we could harness it. (Imagine a perfect world where a million marbles roll down the side of a mountain to power a trolley that transports the same marbles back to the top of the mountain. Utopia!)

I run at night because the streets are emptier and there's less chance of bumping into someone I know. Plus, there's something about running down the street dressed in what has normally been my sleep attire—sweatpants and a Canada's Wonderland sweatshirt—that makes me feel like I'm running away from my woes, escaping a burning house of troubles in the middle of the night. Jogging is good for the heart, but it can also be good for the soul.

MONDAY.

Walking home from work, I spot one of the most masculine-looking men I've ever seen—a construction worker who looks more like Henry Rollins than Henry Rollins. The lines in his forehead appear to have teeth and, to top it off, he's wearing a hard hat and chewing on what appears to be a matchstick.

Inhabiting the same universe as this man is enough to make me feel like a prepubescent Mia Farrow.

At home I phone Gregor.

"I fear I haven't enough machismo," I say. "I bear not even a passing resemblance to any of the masculine stereotypes outlined by the Village People—construction worker, cowboy, biker—not a one."

"Wasn't there a passive-aggressive accountant?" he asks. "Wore a cardigan with torn-off sleeves? Carried a leather abacus board?"

"I need to make some changes," I say.

"You can't turn a taco into a burrito."

"Sure you can," I say. "You just pack more stuff in there."

"Pack too much in a taco and it breaks. Burritos have bottoms."

"I have a lovely bottom. Some say it's the rump of a Greek god."

"If you really want to be more macho," Gregor says, "you might want to stop talking about your 'lovely bottom.'"

Since a bottom as lovely as mine doesn't stay that way by merely being sat upon, I set out for an evening run.

ON BEING THE FASTEST RUNNER: THE HARE RETORTS

———◆———

Honourable animals of the forest counsel, Secretary Otter and Chairperson Skunk, I'm sorry but I must interrupt. I know that time is of the essence, so I'll keep my remarks brief.

I stand before you not an arrogant hare, nor a flashy hare as some of you would have it, but merely a hare who cares about this forest and its creatures.

I've not come to cast aspersions on The Tortoise. This is not a time for partisanship. Whether you be a Hare man or a Tortoise man, we must all work together. To save the forest from its impending doom, it's important that you know the truth about the race known as "Tortoise vs. Hare," or as the tabloids put it in bold sixteen-point headlines, "Tortoise Beats Showboat Hare in Upset of the Decade."

The fact of the matter is The Tortoise cheated.

I know how this makes me look. The Hare is a poor loser, you say. The Hare has a problem with tortoises. Well, I'll stop you right there. Let the record show that I've nothing against turtles of any kind. The Snapping Turtle is godfather to twenty-seven of my kids, for crying out loud.

But if you think there's any chance that Tortoise beat me fair and square, you are deluding yourselves. Tortoises don't just have a "reputation" for being slow. They haven't been "socially conditioned" to *think* the're slow. They *are* slow. Everyone knows this. It's not a question. It's not debatable. It just is.

So imagine my surprise when one morning I wake up to discover the entire forest is talking about how *I* challenged The Tortoise to a race. Think about it: Why would a hare challenge a tortoise to a race? It doesn't make sense. What would it prove? If I win, I'm an asshole; if I lose, I'm an embarrassment to my species.

I should have had my head read for agreeing to it in the first place. I guess I wanted to be a good sport. I guess I wanted you all to like me. Fat chance of that. Oh, how I was vilified after that race! In the picture they ran on the cover of the *Forest Post* I'm pulling my whiskers out, stomping on my top hat, and yelling at a judging official. There I was—the arrogant, buck-toothed hare with the fabulous libido that everyone loves to hate—finally receiving my comeuppance.

And the lies that were told about the race itself! Why would I stop just shy of the finish line and eat a large turkey dinner with all the trimmings? Or why would I pull out a beach chair and take a suntanning break? First of all, I burn easily, and second—what am I, an idiot?

In the days after the race, when I put forth my multiple tortoises in multiple forest nooks theory, I was labelled a paranoid. A conspiracy nut. Not to mention a speciesist for suggesting that tortoises all look the same. But I knew then as I know now that there was a network of them—tortoises, all working in cahoots, stationed behind trees, hiding in briar patches all along the racing route.

Nonetheless, The Tortoise was awarded the title of fastest in the forest, and I'd no choice but to shake his wrinkled green hand and congratulate him.

But dear fellow forest-dwellers, back to the business of this emergency meeting. As Smokey Bear alerted us this morning, the forest is burning. And with all due respect to the authority of this counsel, sending The Tortoise as messenger to tell the creatures of these woods that a fire is raging and they must run for their lives—not the best choice in the world.

The Tortoise left three hours ago, but if you rise up onto your toes, you can still see him creeping along, down at the bottom of the hill.

So he cheated. Who among us hasn't? Possum's cheated at checkers. Fox's cheated on his taxes. And I'm the first to admit that because of my own arrogance, I've cheated myself out of your friendship. And also I've cheated with some of your wives. The point is, we can no longer let this Tortoise charade go on. If we don't do something now, lives will be lost.

So just give me the okay to get running, and as soon as I pick up my top hat at the blockers, fill my jogging pipe with tobacco, and get my retainer inserted, I'll be on my way.

All in favour say "aye." For the love of this forest and all that is good, please say aye.

Sing the Tune Without the Words
(10 weeks)

MONDAY.

Tony stops by for coffee.

"I broke the one-thousand-friend mark on Facebook today," he says. "That's over three times the population of the high school I went to. Do you know how popular the teenage me would have thought the adult me was?"

"Do you feel popular?"

"Not really," he says dejectedly. "Out of that thousand, probably not one would pick me up at the airport or help me move."

TUESDAY.

Nostalgic for the past, I take my yearbook off the shelf and page through it. To complement my wallowing, I head to a Dunkin' Donuts to read while eating Munchkins.

I study my photo. So fresh faced. Favourite quote: "Ain't no thing but a chicken wing." Ah, the wing of the chicken! Like my own hopes, it was the thing that once had feathers.

I get up to order more Munchkins and leave my high school yearbook in the booth. With any luck, it'll have been stolen by the time I get back, and I'll be able to dine without a lump in my throat.

THURSDAY.

Marie-Claude and Helen stop by. Helen offers me some gum. It's green.

"In my day, green meant spearmint," I say. "Now it can mean anything from 'extra cool granny smith apple' to 'outrageously sour lime.' To assure people my age that we don't have to fear cardiac arrest after a few chews, Trident now advertises its peppermint flavour as being 'less intense'!"

Helen inches away.

"You're becoming an old crank," Marie-Claude says.

"Like Walt Whitman," I say defensively, "I celebrate myself, and sing myself."

"But unlike Walt Whitman—you're not Walt Whitman."

Down the Aisle

(9 weeks)

FRIDAY, 7:00 A.M.

Waking up this morning, it occurs to me that if grade school went on forever, I'd now be in grade thirty-four. As a function of seniority, I'd have one of the nicest lockers in the school—close to the cafeteria and roomy enough for all my cholesterol pills.

But school doesn't go on forever, and people get married. People like Tony, even. Of whom, a group of us are planning to show up at his house this evening. To kidnap him. For his bachelor's party.

6:30 P.M.

As a group, we lack the organizational skill to pull off an actual "throw him in the trunk" kidnapping, and so the whole thing has a rather perfunctory feel. We show up in the evening, ring the doorbell, and Natalie invites us in for coffee and cake.

"The wedding's tomorrow and I haven't written my vows yet," Tony says once we're outside. "I was going to write them tonight."

"Just get some vows off the internet," says Tucker.

7:05 P.M.

At the Kart-O-Mania go-cart racetrack we squeeze our heads into ill-fitting helmets. We are shown a three-minute safety video, none of which we can hear because of the skin-tight helmets. Finally, we are given cars and released onto the track.

My go-cart driving style owes something to my Pac-Manning style: I drive aggressively but with hesitation, toggling between flooring the gas and slamming on the brake. This leads to my being waved over by an employee.

My sense of shame at being reprimanded by a seventeen-year-old track attendant for not obeying the rules of go-cart road safety is outdone only by my sense of fear that I will die on a go-cart track. I can only imagine how the obituary would read.

After an evening of racing, cigar smoking, eating, drinking, and then eating some more, it's 3:00 a.m. We drop Tony off and watch him stagger up his front walk.

"Now go write those vows," says Tucker out the car window as we drive off.

SATURDAY.

The wedding is at a country sugar shack, and so Howard regales our group with tales of sugarings-off past.

"One time, a man I didn't even know offered me five hundred dollars to drink an entire jug of maple syrup."

"Talk about an indecent proposal," I say.

"I declined," Howard says.

"Regret it?" I ask.

"On some days," he says wistfully.

All the while, off in the corner, Tony is hunched over some papers. It appears he is still trying to get his vows written.

The caterers have provided branches for the wedding-goers to roast their own marshmallows, but the kids have monopolized them all. Josh complains about the situation and I gesture to the trees around us.

"I know you're not much of an outdoorsman," I say, "but we are in the middle of a forest, and that is where branches come from."

"I don't want a dirty branch," he says sheepishly. "I want a nice clean wedding branch."

I'm about to ask him if he's considered eating his marshmallow raw, as there is a culinary movement that celebrates that sort of thing, but the ceremony is about to begin. On the way to the altar, I reintroduce myself to Tony's Greek mother, whom I haven't seen in years.

"You used to call me The Alley-Cat-Haired Jew," I say, and she nods in recognition.

After the band finishes playing, the vows begin, and I find myself really worried for Tony.

"Love means holding your hand, even when I'm not next to you," Natalie says, going first. "It means striving to be a better person, for both of our sakes. I vow to grow old with you, and most importantly, to grow young with you."

"Me too," Tony responds, his eyes welling up with tears. "Me too."

The Levy Equation

(8 weeks)

SUNDAY.

It's six o'clock in the evening and I've just woken from a four-hour nap. Rather than feeling refreshed, I feel discombobulated, depressed, and nauseated. I head out for coffee.

The man who works at the coffee shop near my house bears a striking resemblance to Eugene Levy, but the thing is, he's nothing like Eugene Levy. I dislike him for the way he scowls and grumbles while making espresso, yet I know that I would not judge him nearly as harshly if he did not look so much like Eugene Levy. It's unfair, but I'm always let down by the discrepancy between his Eugene Levy looks and his un-Eugene-Levy-like behaviour. As I await my coffee, I realize that my dislike of the coffee counterman is inversely proportional to my love of Eugene Levy. Also, the counterman makes one of the best coffees in the city, and so it's as though his bitterness is directly proportional to the quality of the coffee he makes. I'm sure these thoughts can be expressed through an equation, but I'm not sure what it would be.

MONDAY.

I've again awoken from an early evening nap and again, I set out for coffee. I am queasy with dread and my cheek bears the imprint of the bedspread. I cannot bring myself to enter Eugene's, so I head to the other coffee shop next to it.

The man in line in front of me is wearing one of those leopard-skin do-rags. He has a dagger earring hanging from his ear and pleather pants. Despite all this outlaw stuff, he asks the woman at the counter if he can have a "mocha jazz" flavoured coffee.

I figure that for Do-rag, everything must be flavoured. Never the regular kind of anything. Never plain potato chips—always barbecue or salt and vinegar. I envy how everything for him is a showcasing of the brightly burning soul within himself.

When it's my turn, I ask what mocha jazz is.

"The 'mocha' part I get," I say to the woman behind the counter, "but what's the 'jazz'?"

"It's just a name," she says. She seems sort of annoyed.

She hands me my coffee and I say, "Merci, Madame." I've been trying to wean myself from the word "Madame" lately, but it's not easy. Josh says that calling a woman "Madame" is like saying "m'lady."

I wonder if she thinks I'm a sarcastic creep.

WEDNESDAY.

I've been dreading this day for years. The time has come to renew my passport. I study my new passport photo. A sad-looking bearded man in front of a white backdrop. Maybe letting my beard grow back wasn't such a great idea. What is it about beards and sadness that they go so well together? It's like the tears flowing down your cheeks make the beard grow especially lush.

There's comfort in a sad beard, too. It's like you're expressing something. Resignation, perhaps. Plus, it makes you feel like part of an illustrious tradition of sad, bearded men who have come before. The older, fatter Jim Morrison, the bedridden Brian Wilson, and the spider-holed Saddam Hussein.

I phone Marie-Claude.

"Men have beards," I say. "What do women have for their sadness?

"Much of our sadness is caused by men's beards," she says.

After a brief conversation, I put the phone down and go shave. After all, there's already enough sadness in the world.

In the bathroom, I look at myself in the mirror. What

would my life become if I stopped in mid-shave, with a moustache, and walked off into the world? Is this how you become a certain kind of person? You start off just wanting to check something out for a moment, but then you keep stretching that odd, moustachioed moment out longer and longer, until one day, you look in the mirror and a moustache isn't so odd anymore—it's simply a part of your life. Maybe that's all a life is—an accumulation of things that are initially weird and that, over time, become less so. A moustache. A tattoo. A leopard-print do-rag. You bundle all these weird things together to form this even weirder thing: who you are.

I shave off the moustache, feeling good about who I am not, which is close enough to feeling good about who I am.

The Great Rabbi

(7 weeks)

THURSDAY.

In the dream, Boosh has announced she is the reincarnation of the Great Rabbi's beard.

"The Great Rabbi himself?" I ask.

"Just his beard," she says. "That is how a great holy man is dealt with by The Almighty. Each part of him is reincarnated. His nose, each of his fingers—even his fingernails."

"And you are his beard?" I ask.

"Yes," she says.

In the dream, this admission is even odder than the fact she is speaking English.

"And on the day of reckoning," she continues, "when the Great Rabbi returns from the grave, he will come place me in my rightful spot—as the snow-white beard of a wise and holy man."

"And are you wise?" I ask.

"Not really," she says. "Remember how I once asked you why you were collecting my waste in bags?"

"Yes," I say, for in the dream, there is this dream memory. "You didn't realize I was throwing them out."

"I thought you were preserving them in plastic," she says, "like first edition comics. I thought you had hundreds of pounds somewhere, warehoused."

"So, not so wise," I say. "But what can you expect as a beard? A little soup falling your way once in a while? And yet you look forward to this day of reckoning?"

"I think so," she says.

"But won't you miss me?" I ask. "Don't you like living with me?"

"Yes," she says. "And even as a beard, I will think of you often."

In the dream, after hearing this, I scoop her up and hug her to my face. I press my face right into her fur, feeling what it would be like to have a beard so lush, and be a wise and holy man.

I awake to find Boosh asleep on my face.

City Folk
(6 weeks)

SUNDAY.

In the café, the waiter brings me a chicken sandwich on sourdough bread with mayonnaise. I'd ordered a turkey sandwich with mustard on whole wheat. When was it that carrying a notepad to write down orders became archaic?

I think that until waiters start writing things down again, I'm going to start giving my orders in rhyme—as a memory aid.

"Please don't think my rhyming quirky—
Bring me wheat and mustard, betwixt it, turkey."

This is how one becomes what is commonly known as "a character."

TUESDAY.

Tony calls up sounding refreshed after his week-long honeymoon in the country.

"Nature has a way of grabbing you in a headlock and bullying you into a state of bliss," he says.

"Spoken like a modern-day Thoreau," I say. "Did you stay in a cottage? Because, you know, that's where cottage cheese comes from."

"Yes," he says, "and I spent much of the week scraping it off the cottage walls with Melba toast, the way our fore-fathers did. I've even brought some back to sell."

"A cottage industry!"

Tony tells me he needs to get off the phone. He's just not ready for the sassy, ironic bantering of city folk.

FRIDAY.

I'm engaged in what's become my generation's solving of the Rubik's cube—untangling an earbud cord from my keys—when the phone rings. It's Tucker calling to commiserate about his love life.

"I've begun finding washing dishes sensual," he says.

"I find it titillating when the sleeve on my take-out coffee slips down, revealing the hot, naked paper cup."

"For an added touch of eros, you should start referring to the sleeve as a 'coffee skirt.'"

"I wonder how those sleeves caught on."

"So many imbecilic things capture the public imagination," he says. "Sex, for example."

Once our ironic city bantering is done, I get off the phone and continue untangling my earbud cord, sensually undoing each sensuous knot.

A Final Toast

(5 weeks)

MONDAY.

As of today, the cafeteria at work has started charging twenty-five cents for a packet of Melba toast. This spells the end of Melba toast and me.

And I have loved everything about Melba toast: the scraping sound it makes when spread with butter; how sobering the crunch can be. I even loved tearing open the plastic and producing two unbroken, pristine tablets (sometimes I'm tempted to place a little breadstick Moses between them). But above all things, I loved that they were free.

Paying wouldn't be the same. It'd be like paying for flowers instead of picking them from a highway meridian— buying napkins instead of just grabbing a bunch from McDonald's.

Ah, Melba toast! The way you pandered to my cheapness was your secret ingredient.

And also your dextrose.

WEDNESDAY.

Breakfasting on the last of my stored Melba toast over the wastepaper basket in my office, I find myself hearkening back to a time when I thought that wherever I was was where "it was at." As an adult, I've come to see that where I am is where it is not, will never be, and perhaps, never was.

THURSDAY.

I'm shopping for new eyeglasses. Short of surgery, a new pair of glasses is the closest a person ever gets to trying on a new face and starting over. When I've finally found a flattering pair, the saleswoman tells me they are ladies' frames. That they are called "Alex Nicole Pretty Woman Eyeglasses" should have been the tipoff. My next favourite pair are athletic goggles. They make me look so good I consider taking up jai alai as an excuse to wear them.

But as usual, unable to make up my mind, I leave with nothing.

On the bus ride home, I am struck with an idea: car windshields that come in prescription glass. You wouldn't ever have to wear glasses while driving, and thieves couldn't steal your car. Unless they're near-sighted, but I'm reasonably certain most car thieves are not.

FRIDAY.

I'm studying my face in the mirror, and considering contacts. The good thing about glasses, though, is that they cover the bags under your eyes. They say that at forty, a man has earned his face. At thirty-nine, I hope my fate hasn't yet been sealed, that I can still slip a few changes in under the wire. Maybe it's not too late to spend a few weeks grinning like an idiot to ensure a few laugh lines. Or at the very least, a relaxing stay in a sanatorium.

Musical Chairs

(4 weeks)

THURSDAY.

Before exercising at the Y, I usually stretch by a window while making excruciating eye contact with the old man who lives across the street. He keeps a pillow on the windowsill of his third-floor apartment so that he can get some good leaning, spitting, and staring done. But today, rather than endure what I can't help but feel to be his silent judgment, I watch the five-year-old campers play musical chairs in the centre of the gym.

The plight of the odd man out—running around looking for a seat and then slowly realizing there is none, that it's all too horribly late—is heartbreaking to watch. It's as though, through play, the children are being prepared for the cruelty of life and career to come. All to the strains of Nicki Minaj.

FRIDAY.

I can't get the sight of those kids from the Y out of my head. I share my melancholy with Gregor when he stops by my office to discuss "opportunities."

"I was excellent at musical chairs," he says. "I was a precocious kid. At my age now, being precocious would mean lying down in a coffin and awaiting interment."

In recompense, Gregor offers to take us for hot dogs, but I decline.

"I've been feeling a little heart–attacky lately," I say.

"If your life was ever made into a police drama, it'd be called *Scaredy Cop*."

"Fine," I say. "I'll go."

When we get to the snack bar, there's only one open stool at the counter. Gregor takes it, leaving me to stand. In life you may not always get a seat, but often there are hot dogs to make your stand more bearable.

Social Studies

(3 weeks)

SUNDAY.

While visiting my father in the suburbs, I tag along for his daily walk.

"A little exercise will do you good," he says while stretching. It's a procedure that involves bending his knees, cracking his knuckles, and making faces.

The walk, which he's been doing for years, consists of laps around the perimeter of the park across from his house. As we promenade, we keep passing the same fanny-pack-wearing senior citizens over and over. Every time we pass them, they nod to my father and he nods back.

"Everyone's going in the opposite direction," I point out.

"I like to go clockwise," he says. "It's the right way."

"But we're going counter-clockwise."

My father disagrees and we argue the point over the

course of two full counter-clockwise laps. Finally, he stops and closes his eyes. He imagines he is above us, floating in the clouds, looking down on the earth and trying to read a park-sized wristwatch. Then he concedes.

"All this time I've been going the wrong way," he says dejectedly. "What these people must think of me!"

"They probably just think you're a free spirit," I say. "A rebel forcing society to confront its buttoned-down, clock-wise ways. Anyway, if you want, let's just switch."

"I can't switch now," he says, shaking his head reso-lutely. "I'm the kind of guy who stays the course."

And I'm the kind of guy who doesn't really care one way or the other, so together we walk on, against the clock, nodding to the neighbours, feeling our muscles, as well as our character, grow bigger and stronger with each lap.

WEDNESDAY.

Tucker shows up at my office because he "needed a reason to put on pants."

"Why's there a sheet of fabric softener in your garbage?" he asks.

It had been stuck to the back of my sweater all day. When I finally discovered it, I felt like I hadn't a true friend in the office.

"I brought it from home," I say, not entirely lying. "It's like potpourri. A sheet of Bounce and some orange peels in the trash really sweetens up an office."

"Then why's the place still smelling like boiled eggs?" he asks.

"I had eggs for lunch."

Studied or ignored. Each can be painful in its own way.

THURSDAY.

While riding home on the bus, I pull off the headphones I've recently bought to readjust them. In so doing I discover that, due to their open design, the backs of the ear cups have been acting as speakers. What this means is that, unbeknownst to me, I've been sharing my music with everyone.

The idea that a busload of strangers has been able to judge me for my musical taste—examine me as I listen to "Dancing Queen" in the supposed privacy of my headphones—is mortifying. I review a long list of the public humiliations I've endured since the purchase, and stop myself after yesterday's crowded elevator ride while listening to "Eye of the Tiger" for fear of inducing an anxiety attack.

Private music made public, walking against the foot traffic—this is what makes living among humans such a challenge. Society is a bunch of people who can perceive you in a way that you cannot perceive yourself.

I put the headphones back on and press play. I meet the gaze of the teenagers sitting opposite me. I tell myself that my new headphones are character-building as I lower the volume.

Another Lap Around

(2 weeks)

MONDAY.

I've flown to New York for the week, and the hotel I'm staying at has a scale in the bathroom called the "Health o Meter."

When the Health o Meter goes full circle, after it reaches 280 pounds, it still offers little numbers for the second lap around. So underneath the 10, 20, 30, and onward, in finer print, it offers the numbers 290, 300, etc.

What I like about this is that if you weigh 280, you don't have to feel like the heaviest man the Health o Meter serves. You can look at those numbers that come afterwards and think, "I may be heavy—but there are some *really* heavy guys out there." For this reason, I feel that scales should go all the way into the thousands. Why not? To some extent, life is all about looking for whatever you can to make you feel like you're not the last stop—not the heaviest, not the worst, not the oldest—that there is always "some guy" out there. This might account for the popularity of reality television.

TUESDAY.

While browsing in a bookstore, I discover a book about learned optimism and decide to take the test inside. It's composed of forty-eight questions designed to show where one falls on the optimism–pessimism spectrum.

I spend the better part of an hour thoughtfully answering questions like: "You fall down while skiing; a) Skiing is difficult, or b) The trails were icy." Having never been skiing, I answer a). (It turns out that the right answer is b).) When I'm finished I consult the scoring key, and after much calculation and recalculation, I finally accept the book's final assessment. I am what it terms "moderately hopeless."

At first I am saddened, but later I come to a happier conclusion: moderate hopelessness can't really be that different from moderate hopefulness. Is the man half-filled with hope or hopelessness? I'd like to think hope, and in this way I believe myself to be making progress: I am becoming more optimistic about my pessimism.

WEDNESDAY.

In line for a hamburger, I eavesdrop on the teenager ordering in front of me.

"A hamburger," he says. "No onions."

His order captures the heartbreaking optimism of youth. "Maybe I'll meet someone tonight. Maybe we'll get close enough for my onionless breath to matter. Maybe I will perfectly execute some high-kicking, fresh-breathed dance and make all those around me gasp."

"One hamburger," I say when it's my turn. "All dressed. To go."

Conversely, my order conveys the heartbreaking pessimism of adulthood. I don't even ask for napkins. Why bother? I've got sleeves.

THURSDAY.

At a café, I order a chocolate chip cookie.

"One cookie is sixty-nine cents," says the woman at the cash. "But three cookies are ninety-nine cents."

"That's okay," I say.

As I walk away with my sad, lonely cookie, I'm reminded of Ambrose Bierce's definition, from his early 1900s *Devil's Dictionary*, of an abstainer: "a weak person who yields to the temptation of denying himself a pleasure." The book contains no definition of a person who yields to a third of a pleasure.

If I were to write a dictionary of definitions that pertains to my own life, it would include such words as *time* ("that which is always there to assure me I am late"), *moderately hopeless* ("one who purchases a sixty-dollar warranty for a three-hundred-dollar radio, and, in anticipation of getting his money's worth, anxiously awaits its malfunction"), and, of course, *moderately hopeful* ("one who orders his hamburgers with onions on the side, so that in case things don't work out, there's at least onions for later").

As I finish the last bite of my cookie, I am reminded of yet another definition that could go in the book—"cookie: an object that when eaten in singularity can produce dreadful yearning."

I get up and buy a second sixty-nine-cent cookie and, being the foolish, moderately hopeful creature that I am, I do not consider partaking of the special. This despite the fact that both the cashier and I know I'll be back once again, probably within the next several minutes, for a third.

Face to Face
(1 week)

SATURDAY, 10:00 A.M.

Having returned home from New York after midnight, I wake up late and walk into the living room to watch cartoons. Boosh, asleep on the couch, is stirred awake. No sooner does she achieve consciousness than she is growling at me.

"Booshie," I say, my voice slipping into the easy falsetto of a man addressing a poodle in the privacy of his own home, "don't you even know me anymore?"

In reply, Boosh lets loose a series of barks, yips, and snarls that make me feel like a hobo trying to steal pie off a windowsill.

I turn around and leave the room and she settles back into the couch. I should probably wash my face and get ready for the day anyway. That dog brings out the best in me.

10:15 A.M.

While brushing my teeth, I stare at myself in the mirror with great intensity. Sometimes I fear that Boosh can see through me—through the thin veil of niceties and pretend goodness that fools friends and family—to my soul.

10:25 A.M.

I've been staring at myself in the mirror far too long and have entered into a dangerous game: trying to see, without sentimentality, what other people see when they look at me.

As a teenager I would lock myself in the bathroom and stare into my own eyes until, through some act of hypnotism, I could no longer recognize that person in the mirror as me. At which point I felt liberated, as if I'd escaped my "me-ness." In that state, I was just another person in the world, born into personhood as my sister had been, as the old Polish butcher who delivered our chicken had been. I could see with clarity how pimply my skin was, how ill-fitting my burgundy turtleneck, and, despite the assurances of well-meaning aunts, how unlike Matt Dillon I actually did look. And like anyone else who wasn't me, I could finally experience the exhilaration of bad-mouthing myself.

10:40 A.M.

I am not as good at this as I was as a teenager, for try as I might, I can still see something in the reflected jumble that is recognizable as "me." I just can't shake the feeling of kinship with the eyes staring back at me. I guess at this point I've just been me too long.

At thirty-nine, it looks like I can safely assume that this kinship will always be there, whether those eyes in the mirror are sunk in an old man's baked apple of a face or even floating free in a soup bowl of formaldehyde in some future sci-fi world. There is a part of my brain that is now hard-wired to leap up and claim ownership, that shouts, perhaps against all good sense, "That's me."

10:50 A.M.

Boosh enters the bathroom. I stop staring at myself and pick her up. She licks my cheek and it feels nice to have someone appreciate my face, even if it's only a poodle looking for breakfast.

Late Bloomers

(40th birthday)

WEDNESDAY.

I boiled eggs for my father and me on Sunday. I used the stopwatch on my wristwatch to make sure they were cooked for the perfect amount of time. Today I see that the stopwatch is still going. It reads seventy-four hours, twelve minutes, and forty-three seconds. Knowing precisely how long it's been since I boiled eggs for my father and me fills me with a sudden sadness about the passing of time.

FRIDAY, 8:00 A.M.

The plan is to drive down to a rest stop in Newburgh, New York, find a hotel room for the night, and then drive back as early as I can to get to Montreal to host my fortieth birthday party.

Having a rest stop as a point of destination feels odd, but I'm headed there to meet up with the producers of the radio show *This American Life*. I'm joining them there for the day to document a place that most people don't even think of as a place so much as somewhere on the way to getting there.

I'm turning forty at the stroke of midnight, and it feels appropriate that it should happen along a highway connecting New York, the place where I was born, and Montreal, the place where I may very well die.

Beethoven plays on the car radio and the music lends my interior monologue about mortality a certain grandeur. Even my thoughts about whether the rest stop will have a Roy Rogers restaurant become imbued with the collective yearning of an entire species.

11:00 A.M.

I stand in the parking lot and look for people to interview. I feel like a teenager at a high school dance, too afraid to approach anyone for fear of being rejected.

A microphone is a bit like a magic wand. Once it's waved, it makes social conventions vanish, allowing you to ask anything you want of anyone. All it takes is the audacity to wave it.

11:30 A.M.

I take the plunge and approach a dad with his three young sons. I ask him which of the three has to sit in the middle and he points to his eldest.

"I have no choice," the boy says, motioning to each of his brothers. "They'll kill each other without me between them."

"They can probably use a guy like you in the Middle East," I say. "Have you ever considered becoming a diplomat someday?"

"I thought about it," he says, treating the question with great seriousness, "but I think I'd rather become a clown."

3:15 P.M.

A single mom driving to Lake George with her nine-year-old son, Paul: "These trips are the only times we ever get to have long talks."

Sitting in the back seat with nothing to do gives Paul time to hatch questions like, "How long would you cry for if I died?" and "Are you ever sorry you married Dad instead of your old boyfriend?"

She says she always tries to answer him honestly, but as he gets older, it becomes harder. During today's drive he asked if she was really Santa. She told him she wasn't and he said he knew it, but she thinks he was just trying to save face.

8:00 P.M.

A group of women out for a bachelorette party. The bride-to-be has no idea where she's being driven.

"All I know is they told me to bring a whistle and flip flops."

When I ask her friends if they're just messing with her, they all shake their heads no. I ask the bride-to-be if she wouldn't mind standing a few yards away so she can't hear us. Then, once again, I ask her friends about the flip flops and whistle.

"We're totally messing with her," they say.

12:00 A.M.

"This is the sound of me turning forty," I say into the microphone. It sounds like rain beginning to fall, the passing of cars and trucks, of life whizzing by. I feel a lot like that bride-to-be who doesn't know where she's going but has faith it's worth getting to and has faith the people who love her won't, in the end, steer her wrong. Maybe we're both not going to get where we thought we would, but surprises are nice, too.

SATURDAY, 6:00 A.M.

I drive back to Montreal to prepare. The last real birthday party I had was when I was six. My mother got the idea for a party game where you had to pop a balloon as fast as you could to get the pretzel inside. I was freaked out by the idea of hearing a balloon pop, let alone popping one myself. When it was my turn, I sat on my balloon. And nothing happened. I just sort of rolled around on it, pressing down as hard as I could, initially anxious about the popping but eventually concerned that it never would, that I was too tiny and unimportant to make it happen.

After a great deal of laughing from the other kids, my father came over and stepped on the balloon with his loafer. He then scooped up the crushed pretzel and offered it to me.

Over a dinner of hot dogs and chips, my friend Craig Huss wouldn't stop teasing me about needing my father's help, so I poured a glass of orange juice over his hot dog and my mother sent me to my room. It was probably only for a few minutes, but it felt like I was in there the whole party. I still remember how it felt to be lying on my bed and listening to my own party through the closed bedroom door.

I think I'm just about ready for another try.

5:30 P.M.

As guests arrive, I find myself wandering from conversation to conversation. As a result, I catch only snippets.

In the kitchen, Howard and Tony look like they're deep in meaningful conversation.

"We're playing a game," Tony explains when I walk over. "I just invented it. It's called 'Cozy or Claustrophobic.' Like, for instance: a coffin?"

"Claustrophobic," Howard says.

"Okay," Tony answers, taking mental note. "How about a coffin with a teddy bear inside."

"Cozy," says Howard.

I refill their glasses and inch away.

6:45 P.M.

I wander onto the balcony.

"I'd been hearing people talk about 'stay-cations,'" Josh says. "And I couldn't figure out how such a thing could become so popular."

"It's because of the recession," says Marie-Claude. "People 'stay' at home because that's all they can afford."

"I know that now, but initially I thought it was a 'steak-acation,'" he says. "A vacation where you allow yourself to eat as much steak as you like. It's what I did during my summer holiday and now I've gained six pounds."

"I just learned that 'hump day' means Wednesday," Marie-Claude says.

"What did you think it meant?" Josh asks.

"Something dirty," she says.

"Oh, I've got one," Natalie says. "I just learned where the word 'swag' comes from. It's an acronym for 'stuff we all get.'"

Josh then asks if I'll be giving out any swag. I offer to give him some CDs of my radio show, and he declines.

8:00 P.M.

Tucker is standing by himself, staring at the dessert table.

"Have you had a piece of birthday cake yet?" I ask.

"No," he says. "It's a little too ornate for me."

"It is birthday cake, you know," I say.

"Yes," he says, "but it looks like a big glop of makeup that fell off the Joker's face."

Nonetheless, he cuts himself a piece and plops it onto his plate.

"Thanks for the effort," I say.

"No problem," he says. "I'm just a great guy."

10:15 P.M.

The party's in full swing. Howard is singing Sinatra into a chicken leg, Tony is smoking a cigar on his back, and Katie and Helen are dressing Boosh up in doll clothes.

Gregor pulls me aside.

"I'd say it's all downhill from here but that would be the wrong expression, because going downhill is easy. It's all uphill. And harder each day. Plus you'll have to wake up and pee much more frequently and with greater urgency. But as you know, I'm an optimist, which is why I recently reached out to a contact I met at an incontinence conference from years ago. Guess who's going to be the new face of adult diapers in North America, excluding Canada and the U.S.? That's right, Signor Continental Incontinence. You."

"I didn't make it," I say. "This isn't where I thought I'd be."

"That's why people have kids," he says, growing sombre. "Before I had mine, my inner monologue was 'What to have for lunch? Ow, my stomach hurts. I shouldn't have had that for lunch. What to have for dinner?' And so on. But now, since having a son, a primordial protectiveness has kicked in. Just today I was crossing the street with him and thought, 'I will kill any driver who tries to jump this light.'"

"But you've always been full of rage," I say.

"Indiscriminate rage," he says. "But now my rage has purpose! Oh, it's a wonderful rage that I hope you'll one day know."

He pauses for a moment.

"At least think about the incontinence thing. A diaper and sombrero could be a good look for you."

SUNDAY, 12:30 A.M.

With Boosh curled into my chest, I fall asleep listening to the sound of my friends still going strong through the bedroom door. All in all, it feels like a pretty good night.

2:10 A.M.

I can't sleep. I get up to find everyone gone and a half-eaten chicken leg floating in the toilet. I pour myself some orange juice and drink a farewell toast to my thirties.

11:00 A.M.

My father comes by for a breakfast of boiled eggs.

"How do you feel about getting older?" I ask. "Because to me, aside from the getting sick and dying part, it doesn't seem so bad."

"About a month ago," my father says, "someone offered me their seat on the metro. It was the first time that's ever happened to me."

"And?"

"I accepted it," he says. "In your forties, fifties, and sixties, you're still competing for those seats."

"I'm pretty good hanging from the straps."

"You know, in some ways, I was looking forward to retirement since I was a kid," he says.

"Did you take to it right away?"

"Not right away," he says. "'What will I do,' I wondered. 'What will I look forward to?' That was scary. That first day, I remember sitting on the couch and looking out the back window. It was autumn and I watched all the kids going back to school, but for me it was a never-ending summer. No more weekends, because now it was all a weekend."

"Was there a turning point?"

"Yes," he says. "It was a foggy day. There was frost on the ground. But it was beautiful. I'd been moping around the house for weeks, and I finally decided to go to the library. I remember making my way there and feeling like I was moving in a specific direction. I was going to the library and whatever book I picked out, I'd have all day to enjoy it. Your mother had left me lunch in the refrigerator. It was chicken from the night before, and I was looking forward to that, too. That day felt like a beginning. There's always a beginning. You just have to figure it out. As time went by I began to figure it out."

Maybe we Goldsteins are late bloomers, only reaching full blossom in retirement. It's early to say, but right now forty is like beginning the second half of a twelve-inch sub: during the first half, you feel like you have all the sandwich in the world, like there will never be a time where you aren't cramming sandwich into your face; but then comes the second half and the end is in sight. If it was a good sandwich, by the last bite you'll want to undo the top button of your pants and lie down. Hopefully in a good way.

After removing the eggs from the water, I remember to turn off the stopwatch. I sit down with my father and with toast, coffee, and orange juice, we enjoy our eggs.

Afterword

by Gregor Erhlich, ex-agent to the star

Having now skimmed the book you hold in your hands, I realize that this should have been the foreword. A foreword was where I could have said, "Before you read this book: PLEASE, READ THIS WARNING!"

Now it's too late.

Jonathan Goldstein is a liar. And that he is a liar needed to be said first. It needed to be said second, third, and fourth. Why? Because it bears repeating. The stuff in this book is conjecture, half-truths that Goldstein twisted into viscous, colourful balloon animals filled with gassy mendacity.

We are talking about my friend here, so I'm not going to come out and say that Goldstein is an evil man with an evil core. Though likely it is evil smelling. I am picturing a custard-like, greyish brown substance that emits a high-pitched whining noise when subjected to the scrutiny of sunlight. I'm just saying he has trouble with reality. Anyone

who's ever been a passenger while he's driving can attest
to that.

And as for you others out there who think Goldstein's
some grand Canadian absurdist with a Victorian birdcage
full of *bon mots* printed on index cards, you are mistaken.
Truth is, he's only *half* Canadian. A *dual* citizen. I'd say that's
reason enough not to trust him right there. I mean, come
on. Choose a country. I did. U.S.A. all the way. You probably
chose your home team, too. But not Goldstein. Goldstein
likes to play both sides of the border.

Still want proof of his deceit? I present to you evidence
from *his own book*! Exhibit A:

> Gregor visits me at my office.
> "What's this?" he asks, pointing to the large
> yoga ball under my desk.

Okay, let's stop right there. I know what a yoga ball is.
I've been familiar with yoga since before it was Upanishadic.
And I know my way around Kundalini, Iyengar, and
Bikram, and have read the *Yoga Yajnavalkya*.

Want more? Here's more:

> "A yoga ball is the rare object that can boast
> having had buttocks pressed against every
> millimetre of its surface. The sphere, my friend.
> Nature's perfect cootie catcher."

Why would I mention "buttocks pressed against every millimetre" when, as noted earlier, I am a one hundred percent, apple pie–eating, missile-firing U.S.A. citizen? I don't say millimeter, and certainly not millimetre. I say foot, pound, and inch. And any mention of the four-thousand-dollar Bruno Magli shoes I was wearing? The one-thousand-and-ninety-dollar aftershave? I hardly recognize myself! We continue, back into his dank cabinet of dissemblance:

> "I guess that's why it's the perfect shape for a place
> that's home to asses like us."

He wanted to make his stupid joke about the Earth—which, by the way, is one of my top favourite planets. In fact, had he dared muse this in front of me—like a man, and not some mouse creeping around musing behind people's backs—I might well have punched him in the eye.

You read this book thinking you'd experience the balancing of a man's soul, and instead you've a book barely worth using to balance out a chair leg. Goldstein remains the same potted plant at forty that he was at thirty-nine. He's like the Human Condition come to life.

This was the diary of a turtle. A slow, frightened, reptilian inhabitant of a hard shell carrying God knows what diseases. Now that I think of it, "Diary of a Turtle" kind of rolls off the tongue.

I've learned my lesson and will write the foreword to his next book, *Diary of a Turtle*, once I've acquainted myself with it first. If it's about turning fifty, knowing Goldstein and his "perception" of "time" and "reality," that could be anywhere from twenty to twenty-five years from now. When it happens, I'd suggest buying the hardcover edition. Better for killing spiders.

Acknowledgments

Thanks to all the people who helped make this book better: Sarah Steinberg, Jeff Melman, Alex Blumberg, Ira Glass, Julie Snyder, Jorge Just, Diane Cook, Natasha Vargas-Cooper, Ira Silverberg, Mira Burt-Wintonick, Nicole Winstanley, John Hodgman, Paul Tough, Mireille Silcoff, Sean Cole, Karen Alliston, Ben Errett, Isa Tousignant, Arthur Jones, Alia Hanna Habib, and Shima Aoki.

And thanks to those who find versions of themselves herein. They are all dear to me. This means you, Buzz, Dina, Eileen, Marjie, Justin, Mike, Marie-Claude, Helen, Katie, Starlee, Ruby, Carolyn, Mira, Josh, David, Tony, Natalie, Tucker, and agent of my heart, Gregor Ehrlich. I am especially grateful to Howard Chackowicz, who spoke the title of this book to me while staring at his shoes in a Winnipeg hotel elevator.